MAKING
POLYMER
CLAY
JEWELLERY

MAKING POLYMER CLAY JEWELLERY

Text and illustrations by
SUE HEASER

CASSELL

This edition first published in the UK 1997 by
Cassell
Wellington House
125 Strand
London WC2R 0BB

First paperback edition 1998
Reprinted 1999

Designed by Yvonne Dedman
Photography by Martin Norris

Distributed in the United States by
Sterling Publisher Co. Inc.
387 Park Avenue South
New York, NY 10016-8810, USA

British Library Cataloguing-in-Publication Data
A catalogue record for this book is available from the British Library

ISBN 0 304 35030 3

Typeset in Palatino by
Litho Link, Welshpool, Powys, Wales
Printed and bound in Spain by
Gráficas Reunidas S.A. Madrid

CONTENTS

INTRODUCTION

The last decade has seen the appearance of an exciting new craft medium. Called modelling clay or polymer clay, it is sold under several different brand names, including Fimo, Sculpey, Cernit and Formello. This wonderful material comes in a rainbow of colours and, once modelled, it can be permanently hardened by being baked in a home oven. There is no need for expensive kilns, and the initial outlay on materials is trifling compared with most other crafts. These colourful clays can be mixed with each other to produce further colours, and a multitude of different techniques can be applied to them. Once hardened in the oven, they can be cut, sawn, filed, sanded, glued, painted, added to and re-baked. They are clean and odourless to work with, and non-toxic.

The qualities of these new clays mean that they are ideal for making spectacular jewellery. Once baked, the clays are robust and long-lasting – I have some pieces of jewellery made from polymer clay that I have worn for over ten years and that show no sign of deterioration.

The most exciting aspect of making jewellery using the new modelling clays is that you can create effects in your own home that until now, could be achieved only by metalworkers, silversmiths, potters, woodworkers, ceramicists and jewellers. If it is left unvarnished the clay has a delightful patina, but it can also be used to mimic most of the traditional materials used to make jewellery, such as precious metals, porcelain, wood and stone. A new medium really comes into its own, however, when it is used creatively to develop new techniques that until now have not been possible with conventional materials. Millefiori, metallic effects and porcelain-like flowers are all examples of polymer clay's extraordinary versatility.

Newcomers to the craft will find that the initial techniques are simple and use the skills developed in childhood of rolling and shaping clay or dough. For the more advanced crafter, there are always exciting new skills to try.

POLYMER CLAYS

All the main brands of polymer clay can be used to make the projects in this book. The clays are widely available from art and craft shops and through mail order suppliers, although the availability of different brands varies from one country to another (see page 127 for suppliers).

Whichever brand you use, you will find a wide variety of colours and many brands have special effect clays, which include stone effects, fluorescents, metallics and translucents. The colours can be mixed with each other to produce an unlimited range of new colours. In addition, the different brands can be intermixed, although it is prudent to test samples first and this may affect the durability of the baked clay.

The texture of the clay is very fine, so that detailed modelling is possible, and it can be rolled into thin sheets and draped like fabric, extruded through a machine, or sliced, grated, modelled and sculpted. It can also be tooled and impressed like metal and leather, and coloured with metallic powders and chalks.

The clay remains soft until it is baked, and unused clay, carefully stored, has a shelf life of several years.

The clay is stable when it is baked, and there is very little shrinkage and virtually no colour change.

Once they have been hardened by baking at approximately 130°C (250°F) in a domestic oven, the finished items can be cut, sawn, added to and re-baked, glued, and painted with water-based paints. After hardening, they remain slightly flexible and are durable and robust. They do not reach full hardness until cool.

Fimo

Fimo is manufactured by Eberhard Faber of Germany and is very widely available. The texture is firm, and the material has to be kneaded thoroughly before use to soften it. The firm nature of the clay makes it particularly good for detailed work. Once baked, it is opaque, fairly strong and slightly glossy; thin pieces are flexible.

Other Fimo products:
◆ Mix Quick, which is a mixing agent that can be kneaded into the clay to soften it.
◆ 'Fimo Soft' clay is softer in texture than the original Fimo.
◆ Fimo 'Stone Effect' clays.
◆ Metallic powders in a wide range of colours.
◆ A variety of varnishes especially for polymer clay.

Cernit

Made by T + F GmbH in Germany, Cernit is a medium textured clay and needs some kneading before use. It is a semi-translucent clay with a porcelain-like effect. After baking, it has a slight gloss and thin pieces are flexible and strong. Opaque white can be added to the colours for a more opaque effect if required.

Other Cernit products:
◆ 'Nature's Colours' granite effect clays

Sculpey III

Sculpey III is manufactured by Polyform Products of Illinois, USA. This is a soft clay and requires little initial kneading to make it workable, although it may be too soft for more delicate projects. Once baked, it has an attractive matt texture, but is rather brittle and should not be used where a strong result is needed such as for buttons.

Other Sculpey products:
◆ Granitex granite effect clays

Premo Sculpey

Also manufactured by Polyform Products in the USA, Premo is one of the newer clays. It has a medium texture, kneads up quickly and is good for detailed work. It has an excellent range of colours that are highly saturated and are named after artists' paint colours – a useful attribute when mixing. The baked clay is strong and flexible.

Formello (or Modello in some countries)

Manufactured by Rudolf Reiser in Germany, Formello has a medium texture. The colours are bright and opaque. It can be used for good detail but the baked clay is not particularly strong.

Modelene

Manufactured in Australia, Modelene has a medium texture and kneads up quickly for use. After baking, it is extremely strong and flexible – useful qualities for jewellery.

Du-Kit

A medium textured clay made in New Zealand by Creative Products. It comes in a good range of hues with a useful colour mixing chart. The recommended temperature for baking – 150°C (300°F) – is higher than for most other brands. After baking it is extremely strong and flexible.

Jonco

Produced in Holland by Jonco, this clay is slightly firmer than some other medium-textured clays. It is of medium strength after baking.

Prima

Made in the UK by Peter Pan Playthings, Prima is mainly marketed in boxed sets and kits for children. Slightly crumbly initially, it soon kneads to a soft texture and, after baking, has a chalky feel.

EQUIPMENT

You will probably find all the basic equipment needed to work with polymer modelling clay in your home. As you become more experienced, however, you may want to acquire specialist modelling tools, although I have never found these essential. Because this is such a robust material, it is also possible to make your own tools from the clay itself should you require a particular shape.

The following list includes all the basic tools used for the projects in this book. When specific tools are needed for a particular project, they are described in the instructions for that project.

◆ Board – a smooth melamine chopping board to work on is ideal. Alternatively, use a formica table mat.
◆ Craft knife – a rounded blade (as shown in the photograph opposite) is the most versatile shape. Blunt the blade slightly before use by running it over a steel because razor-sharpness is not necessary for most techniques.
◆ Ruler – you will need to check the size of balls, cylinders and other shapes.
◆ Blunt-ended wool (tapestry) needles – both a large and a small needle are useful. The points are used to make holes and mark lines, while the eyes of the needles mark feathers on a bird or even a clown's smile.
◆ Darning needles and pins – these are used for piercing beads.
◆ Small rolling pin – a smooth barrelled pencil or pen is best for tiny rollings, while a straight-sided glass or small bottle can be used for flattening larger pieces.

◆ Pointed tool – a dried-up ball-point pen with a cone-shaped point is ideal for making eye sockets. Otherwise, a smoothly sharpened but blunted pencil, which has been dipped in varnish to stop the lead marking the clay, can be used.
◆ Artists' paintbrush handles – these are useful rounded tools.
◆ Razor blade – used for slicing millefiori canes; a two-edged blade can be given a guard by pressing a thin log of clay along one edge and baking.
◆ Nail varnish remover – clean your hands and the board with this.
◆ Talcum powder – use ordinary talcum powder for dusting the board and your hands to prevent the clay from sticking.
◆ Aluminium foil – used as a support during baking.
◆ Baking tray – line the tray with non-stick baking parchment.

EQUIPMENT KEY

1. Board	10. Craft knife
2. Rolling pin	11. Paintbrush handles
3. Talcum powder	12. Pointed tool
4. Razor blade	13. Pins
5. Aluminium foil	14. Wool needles
6. Baking tray	15. Darning needle
7. Artists' pastel	
8. Metallic powders	
9. Ruler	

Other Equipment

Other items of equipment can be adapted for use with polymer clay. Here are some suggestions, but you will find many ideas of your own by looking around your kitchen or home.

◆ Biscuit cutters – use them to cut out regular shapes.
◆ Rubber stamps – stamp designs on to sheets of clay.
◆ Clay gun extruders – many craft and hobby shops stock these extruders which will produce lengths of different shapes.
◆ Garlic press – used to form long, thin pieces of clay.

Some clay artists use larger items of kitchen equipment, such as a food processor for the initial kneading of the clay or a pasta machine for rolling sheets, but this is only worthwhile if you are producing large quantities of clay work, because they should never be used for food use as well, and you will need to buy duplicate equipment.

When you use kitchen equipment with clay, remember that you should never use the same utensil for food that you use for clay. Although the clay is non-toxic, it should, nevertheless, never be allowed to come into contact with items used in the preparation of food. Keep your clay tools exclusively for that purpose.

Varnishes

Varnish gives the baked clay a brilliant shine and intensifies the colours. It is, however, not essential to apply a coat of varnish because the clay does not need it for protection as it is durable enough on its own. Many people find that the matt finish of the clay has its own charm, so use varnish only where you require a gloss finish. Matt varnish is available and is useful for protecting painted areas such as faces without giving a shine.

Do *not* use ordinary enamel-based varnish, which will not dry on the baked clay. The manufacturers of some of the main brands of polymer clay make their own water- or spirit-based varnishes, and

these are excellent. Alternatively, water-based acrylic varnish, which is available in craft shops can be used.

Paints

Polymer clay can be successfully painted after baking, but you must first remove all traces of grease from the surface of the clay by brushing it with methylated spirit or nail varnish remover.

Do *not* use enamel or oil paints, because they will not dry on the baked clay. The best paints to use are water-based acrylics, either artists' or hobby paints, which give the most permanent results. Ordinary water-based paint can lift and stain in time, even under a varnish. Protect painted areas with matt or gloss varnish.

Powder Colours

Metallic powders give some really spectacular effects when they are used with polymer clay. Fimo and Cernit both produce a range of metallic powder colours, and although they are quite expensive, they are very economical to use and the results are far superior to metallic paint.

The powder is brushed on to the surface of the unbaked clay with a soft artists' paintbrush. After baking, the clay is varnished to protect the powder.

Other metallic powders of the kind sold in craft shops can be used, and it is even possible to use eye shadow colours, although they vary in their ability to coat the clay, so you need to experiment. Artists' pastels are effective when they are applied on light coloured clays. Rub a little colour on to paper first to release the powder for brushing.

Metallic effects are described in detail in Chapter 6 (page 83).

BASIC TECHNIQUES

In order to avoid constant repetition, the individual instructions for each design assume that you understand these basic techniques. You must, therefore, read the following section before you attempt the designs in this book.

General Hints
Always clean your hands thoroughly before you begin working with clay, because the smallest trace of dirt will be transferred to the clay and stain it. Wiping over with cleansing wipes or nail varnish remover should be sufficient. Remember to cleanse again between colours.

Try to avoid poking and patting the object you are making. Once a piece of clay has been added, do not try to reshape it, or the result will be messy. If you are not happy with it, remove the piece and start again.

It is not necessary to squash pieces together to effect a join – gentle but firm pressure is all that is needed – they will weld together when they are baked in the oven.

Softening the Clay
Before use, always work each piece of clay in your hands to soften it. The amount of kneading required to make clay soft and pliable varies not only between brands but also between colours made by the same manufacturers. Insufficient kneading will result in bubbles and irregularities on the baked surface. If you need a large piece, cut small amounts off the block and work them individually before combining. In cold weather warm the clay gently on a hot-water bottle until it is more pliable. If the clay is crumbly, you have not worked it enough. Fimo, which is one of the hardest of the clays, may be quickly softened by the addition of Mix Quick.

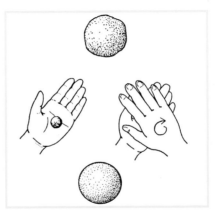

Making Balls
The clay ball is the starting point for many designs, and perfectly round balls are essential for making beads.

Squeeze the clay into a rough ball and then rotate it between your palms, heavier pressure first and then lighter as the ball takes shape.

Many of the projects start with a clay ball of a particular diameter. Using your ruler as a guide, shape a ball roughly the right size and pinch off or add clay as necessary.

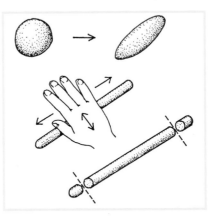

Making Cylinders or Logs
Making cylindrical shapes is an important part of working with clay.

Practise rolling clay into even logs of different thicknesses. Start with a ball of clay and roll it between your hands. Place the resulting oval on your surface and roll it smoothly, making sure that

your hand keeps moving back and forth along the length of the log and that you do not press too hard. Lay logs on a ruler to check that they are the right thickness. Trim off the rounded end and then cut off equal slices with your craft knife to give identically sized pieces of clay.

Because polymer clay is a relatively new craft medium, it has had to develop its own terminology, and the cylindrical shape has been called many different things by different writers, including 'sausage', 'roll', 'log', 'snake' and 'cylinder'. The favoured word appears to be 'log'.

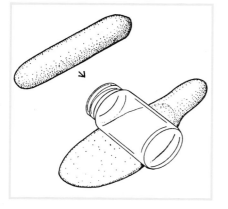

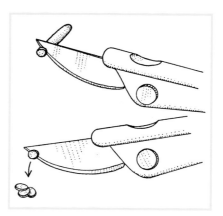

Rolling Sheets of Clay

Some designs require flat sheets of clay, and these are surprisingly easy to make. Form a thick log of clay and press it down on the board, then roll out the clay wih your 'rolling pin' as if it were pastry. You will need a bottle or jam jar as a rolling pin for larger pieces, but small pieces are best rolled with a smooth pencil or pen barrel. Keep some talcum powder handy to dust the surface of the clay if necessary to prevent it from sticking. Larger sheets of clay are best rolled out between two pieces of baking parchment.

Using a Craft Knife

A craft knife with a curved blade is an invaluable tool. Not only is it useful for cutting clay to the required size, but it can also be used as a delicate tool for moving pieces of clay when your hands would soon distort them. Thin slices and tiny strips of clay are best applied by scooping them up on the tip of the knife. They should adhere sufficiently to the knife for you to turn over the blade and place them as required. You can then use it to press them down lightly. This technique is covered in detail in Chapter 7 (page 101).

CLAY COLOURS

The clay used to make the projects illustrated in this book was Fimo, but you can use any of the other brands instead. Because the different manufacturers use different names for the colours in their ranges I have used descriptive rather than proprietary names. The photograph of coloured discs (below) shows all the colours of clay used in this book so that you can match the colours of the brand of clay you want to use.

Mixing Colours

Polymer modelling clays are available in a wide range of colours, and these can be combined to make other shades. This means you can create a large palette of clay colours in much the same way as an artist mixes paint. Making new colours is a simple process – work two or more pieces of coloured clay together until all streakiness has disappeared and the new colour emerges. It is often better to mix a small quantity first so that you can judge proportions.

Many of the colours used in the book can be mixed from a few basic colours, and some suggestions are listed below. Do not be reluctant to mix your own palette of colours; for example, if you have dark brown and white clays, there is no need to buy light brown because it can be mixed simply by combining brown and white. Instructions for further blends of colour are included in the projects where necessary.

Colours Used in the Projects

1. White	11. Turquoise
2. Transparent	12. Leaf green
3. Black	13. Light brown
4. Red	14. Ochre
5. Yellow	15. Grey
6. Green	16. Orange
7. Blue	17. Golden-yellow
8. Violet	18. Pink
9. Crimson	19. Flesh
10. Dark brown	

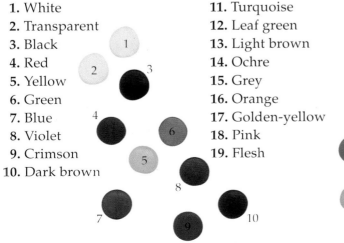

All of these colours, or their close equivalents, are available in the main brands of polymer clays. For economy, colours 11 to 19 can be mixed from the first 10 colours as follows:

11. Turquoise = green + blue
12. Leaf green = green + trace of brown
13. Light brown = brown + white
14. Ochre = white + brown + yellow
15. Grey = white + trace of black
16. Orange = yellow + trace of red
17. Golden-yellow = yellow + trace of orange
18. Pink = white + trace of crimson or red
19. Flesh = transparent + trace of brown + trace of red

When a precise colour mixture is needed in a project, the proportions of the different colours of clay required to make a particular colour are given in the instructions. For example, pink = 1 red + 8 white.

This means you need to mix 1 part red with 8 parts white. To do this, roll a 6mm (¼in) log of red and another 6mm (¼in) log of white. Cut eight equal lengths of white and one, the same length, of red. Mix these together to create pink.

Where no proportions are given, the colour balance is less critical, and you should mix to your own taste.

When you are mixing pastel shades, add small quantities of coloured clay to white until you have the colour you require; you will need far more white than colour. Remember that darker clays are stronger and will dominate. For example, you will need far less red than yellow when you are mixing orange.

Some lovely effects can be obtained by mixing a transparent white with a colour to create a translucent effect, rather like porcelain. Cernit has this translucent effect in all colours.

Mix smoky shades by combining a colour with a small quantity of black.

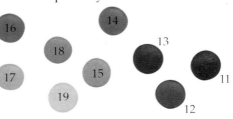

Marbling

This is an easy technique that will enable you to produce some stunning results. You can combine bright colours for a flamboyant effect or mix subtle colours with black and white to represent semi-precious stones. First, form logs of the colours you want to marble. Press, then roll, these logs together to make one long log. Now fold this up several times and roll again. Continue until the resulting stripes are as thick as you want but do not continue too long, or they will disappear completely into one new colour.

Try out different combinations of colours and different proportions of each. If you coil a marbled log and form it into a ball, for example, this will give curls and loops among the stripes. Transparent colour mixed with opaque also looks very effective, but experiment because the variety is endless.

STORAGE

Polymer modelling clay has a shelf life of several years – I have eight-year-old clay that is still workable. In time it will dry out and become crumbly, and heat and light will accelerate this process. Unopened packets should be stored in a cool, dark place, while opened clay is best kept in a tin or wrapped in plastic bags. Unbaked clay will exude plasticizer, which can damage polished surfaces or plastic, so take care where you leave your clay.

BAKING

Before baking, remove your designs carefully from the board by slicing under them with the craft knife. Place the clay on a baking sheet that has been lined with baking parchment. All the polymer clays listed should be baked in the oven for about 20 minutes at 130°C (250°F), but always check the manufacturer's instructions first. Larger pieces will need longer, as will designs, such as buttons that

you wish to be particularly strong. The instructions for the projects suggest baking times.

It is advisable to check your own oven's temperature with a special oven thermometer to make sure that the temperature setting is accurate. Oven thermostats vary quite widely, and if clay is baked at too high a temperature, it will burn and may give off toxic fumes. If the temperature is too low, the clay will take a long time to harden or may remain fragile.

Clay will not harden until it is completely cool, but it can be replaced in the oven and baked again if you are not satisfied with the hardness. There may be a slight discoloration of pale colours after prolonged baking.

SAFETY

Polymer clays are all made from fine PVC particles suspended in plasticizers, and it is these that give the clay its malleability and softness. Baking the clay causes the particles to fuse together into a permanent plastic, which is a stable product, but there may be traces of plasticizer left, and these may continue to leach out. All the proprietary clays are called non-toxic, but, as with any art and craft medium, it is sensible to follow some basic precautions as listed below.

◆ **Never allow the clays to overheat.** When they burn, they produce toxic fumes. If you accidentally let the clay overheat, turn off the oven at once and ventilate the room thoroughly. Avoid breathing any fumes.
◆ **Always wash your hands after using polymer clays.**
◆ **Do not allow polymer clays to come into contact with foodstuffs,** even after they have been baked.
◆ **Do not use the same utensils for polymer clays and for food.**
◆ **Supervise young children when they are handling the clays.**

JEWELLERY FINDINGS

Findings are the bits and pieces of metal that you attach to your designs to make them into wearable pieces of jewellery. The terminology can be bewildering, so some of the most useful items are illustrated on page 18 to help you choose exactly what you need.

Glass and metal findings can be attached before hardening if necessary, because they will not be harmed by the baking process, but anything made of plastic or acrylic must be added after baking.

Findings are made with various finishes, of which silver plated or gold plated are the most readily available. These are indicated by SP or GP in the projects. Solid silver and gold findings are also available. The most economical way to buy findings is by mail order from one of the specialist jewellery companies, which advertise in craft magazines. Fimo produces a range of findings, and these can usually be found on sale with the clay and include some that are specially designed for using with polymer clay.

In addition, there are many other findings available – including key rings, stick pins, bracelets and tie pins – that can have a clay design mounted on to them.

General Findings

◆ Eyepins – these are useful for embedding in the clay before baking to provide an attachment point for earrings and pendants.
◆ Headpins – mainly used for threading beads on to earrings.
◆ Jump rings – small split rings, available in various sizes, for attaching clasps, pendants and so forth.
◆ S-fittings – useful for linking jewellery and attaching pendants.
◆ Peg and loop – glue into a hole in the clay to provide an attachment point.
◆ Triangle bails – another useful type of attachment.
◆ Pendant mounts – used to attach pendants to chains or thongs. Squeeze the prongs together into a hole in the clay.

◆ Pendants – milled or plain cup designs into which clay can be pressed.
◆ Brooch backs – various lengths and designs are made. A useful size is 2.5cm (1in). Glue to the back of brooches.
◆ Chain – available in various lengths and styles, such as curb, trace and so on.
◆ Wire – comes in various thicknesses and finishes, of which 0.6mm or 0.8mm are good all-purpose sizes for linking beads and making loop earrings.
◆ Hair clips/barrettes – various sizes are made. Designs can be glued on to create attractive hair ornaments.
◆ Rings – adjustable rings with flat pads or milled cups.

Necklace Fastenings

◆ Bolt ring – used with a jump ring to fasten a necklace.
◆ Torpedo clasp – screw clasp for fastening a necklace.
◆ Calotte crimp – used to enclose the knot at the end of a string of beads and to provide an attachment point for the clasp or jump ring.
◆ Spring end – squeezed on to the end of cord or leather thong to provide attachment for clasps and so on.
◆ Lace end – used in the same way as a spring end.
◆ Hook – useful for fastening leather thong; attached to spring or lace ends.

Necklace Stringing Materials

◆ Leather thong – useful for stringing large beads and pendants, this is available in several colours and thicknesses. Can be knotted to finish or use spring ends and hooks as a fastening.
◆ Cord – comes in a wide range of colours and is used in a similar way to leather thong.
◆ Threads – beads can be threaded on any strong thread e.g., embroidery thread, beading silk and nylon or synthetic bead thread. Remember that clay beads tend to be fairly heavy, so use strong thread.

1
3
2
4
5
6
7
11
12
8
9
13
10
18
14
15
16
17
19
20
21
43
22
23
24
25
26
27
31
16
16
16
28
29
30
32
33
34
35
36
37
38
39
40
41
42
43

Earring Fittings for Pierced Ears

◆ Kidney ear wires – pendant earrings are attached to the loop.
◆ Fish-hook with ball and spring – for pendant or drop earrings.
◆ French ear wire with bead and loop – another pendant style.
◆ Flat pad ear studs – these come in a range of sizes. Clay designs are glued to the pad. The 'butterfly' or 'scroll' is available in plastic for sensitive ears.
◆ Milled cup studs – these are very useful for polymer clay because the clay can be pressed into the cup to make a cabochon or 'stone'.

Earring Fittings for Non-pierced Ears

◆ Flat pad ear clips – the clip version of flat pad ear studs
◆ Ear clip with loops – for use with pendant drops.
◆ Milled cup ear clips – the clip version of milled cup studs.

JEWELLERY FINDINGS AND EQUIPMENT KEY

General findings and beads
1. Chains
2. Jump rings
3. Brooch backs
4. Pendants
5. Semi-precious stones
6. Eyepins
7. Pendant mounts
8. Headpins
9. S-fittings
10. Hair clips
11. Metal beads
12. Metal charms
13. Glass and crystal stones
14. Peg and loops
15. Triangle bails
16. Rocaille beads
17. Bugle beads
18. Liquid silver
19. Liquid gold
20. Wire
21. Rings

Earring fittings
22. Flat pad ear studs
23. Milled cup ear studs

24. Scrolls
25. Flat pad ear clips
26. Ear clips with loops
27. Milled cup ear clips
28. Kidney ear wires
29. Fish-hook ear wires
30. French ear wires

Jewellery making equipment
31. Snipe-nosed pliers
32. Beading needles
33. Scissors

Necklace fastenings and stringing
34. Bolt ring
35. Torpedo clasp
36. Calotte crimps
37. Spring ends
38. Lace ends
39. Hooks
40. Leather thong
41. Embroidery thread
42. Cord
43. Beading thread

Purchased Beads and Stones

It is possible to make complete necklaces out of polymer clay beads but the use of a few purchased beads can provide far more variety and enhance the appearance of your hand-made designs.

◆ Rocaille beads – these tiny glass beads come in a rainbow of colours and finishes. Thread them between larger clay beads to accentuate them.
◆ Bugles – these long, thin glass beads are made in a similar range of colours to rocailles.
◆ Plated metal beads – these come in various sizes and add sparkle to necklaces.
◆ Liquid silver or gold – plated metal, fine tube beads can be either straight or twisted.
◆ Glass and crystal stones – these can be pressed into the clay before baking. Many different kinds are available – from large round cabochons to tiny rhinestones – all in various colours. Fimo produces an excellent range of crystal stones. Do not use plastic or acrylic stones, which will melt during baking.
◆ Other materials – shell pieces, such as paua and abalone, mother-of-pearl, semi-precious stones, little glass mirrors, metal shapes and ceramic, pottery or metal beads will all withstand the low baking temperatures and can be incorporated into designs.

Jewellery Making Equipment

You will need very few tools for applying findings to jewellery. The most useful are listed below.

◆ Pliers – you will need some fine-nosed pliers for attaching findings and making loops. Round-nosed pliers are used to turn loops in the ends of headpins or wire. Flat-nosed pliers are used to close jump rings and attach findings. Snipe-nosed pliers can be used for all tasks, although they do not turn such round loops as round-nosed pliers.
◆ Wire cutters – these are useful if you intend to do a lot of wire work. A pair of old nail scissors can be used for fine wire.
◆ Beading needles – these can be bought from jewellery suppliers or you can make your own (see page 20).
◆ Sharp scissors.

JEWELLERY ASSEMBLY TECHNIQUES

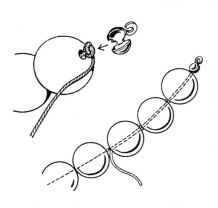

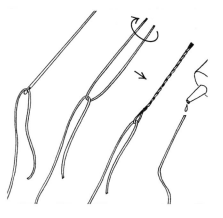

Threading Methods for Necklaces

There are several methods of threading beads:

◆ With a fine beading needle, available from jewellery suppliers.

◆ Using a needle made by twisting a fine piece of wire onto the thread as shown above.

◆ By applying glue to the end of the thread to stiffen it.

Attaching Calotte Crimps

You will need to use pliers to attach calotte crimps. Pinch a calotte crimp tightly over the knot so that the working thread and tail of thread exit through the hole in the bottom of the calotte. Tug gently to make sure that the knot is too large to pull through the hole. Adding a drop of glue to the knot before closing the calotte will make it more secure. Thread the tail of the thread back through the first few beads and trim the end.

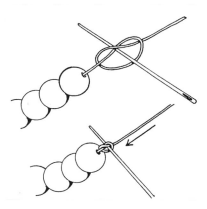

Knotting the Ends of the Necklace

To fasten the ends of a necklace, make a knot in the end of your beading thread, leaving a tail of about 7.5cm (3in). Thread on the beads, then tie a knot as close as possible to the last bead by tying the knot around a needle and sliding it against the final bead as you tighten it. Enlarge the knot if necessary by tying a second knot on top of the first one.

Attaching the Clasps

To attach a torpedo clasp, simply squeeze shut the loops on the clasp over the loops on the calottes. A bolt ring is attached in the same way, with a jump ring at the other end of the necklace. Open a jump ring by pushing one end sideways. If you pull the ends apart, you will find it harder to close them again into a perfect circle.

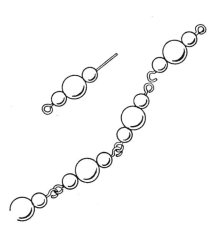

Making Loops

Turning a neat loop in the end of a headpin or eyepin is one of the most frequently used techniques in assembling jewellery. To make drop earrings, for example, a headpin is threaded with beads, and a loop is turned in the end of the headpin to which the finding is attached.

Trim the end of the headpin to 6mm (¼in) from the top bead. Grip the end in your pliers and turn until the loop is formed. Now grip the other side of the loop and turn slightly the other way to centralize the loop and open it a little.

Linking Eyepins with Loops

Necklaces can be made by threading beads on to eyepins, which are then linked together. First, thread the beads on to the eyepins. Trim the eyepins if necessary, before turning a loop in the end of each, and attaching it to the loop of the next eyepin. Squeeze the loop shut.

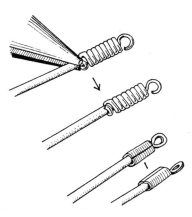

Leather Thong and Cord

Special findings – spring ends and lace end crimps – are used with leather thong and cord. These findings are simple to attach.

Trim the thong to the required length and position the spring end over the end of the thong. Use your pliers to squeeze the bottom coil hard against the thong so that it grips it tightly. A simple hook fastening can then be attached to one end.

Lace ends are squeezed onto the thong so that their sides enclose the thong. A hook is attached in the same way.

Attaching Earring Findings

Attach your chosen finding – kidney wire, fish-hook and so on – and squeeze the loop shut. Close the loops of kidney wires with pliers.

Gluing Findings

Findings such as ear studs, rings and brooch backs need to be glued strongly to the baked clay designs. Remove all traces of grease from both surfaces by wiping them with nail varnish remover. Slightly roughen the surface of the findings with a small file or sandpaper. The surface of the clay can be roughened with an emery board or scratched with a pin.

One of the proprietary superglues or a two-part epoxy glue will give the best results. Superglues are strong and quick setting, but work carefully because they will bond your skin. Use only a tiny spot of glue, just sufficient to give a thin coat on the surface. Hold the two surfaces together for a few seconds, then lay aside to set properly.

Two-part epoxy glues give an extremely strong bond, but they are much slower-setting than superglues. Be careful to mix exactly equal quantities of each part or the glue may not set properly. Mix the two parts thoroughly and apply to one surface. The setting time varies with different glues, but it is usually a minimum of one hour. Try to prop up the jewellery so that the finding is horizontal while the adhesive sets – this prevents it sliding gently off the clay when you are not looking and setting in the wrong place.

THE
PROJECTS

— ◆ —

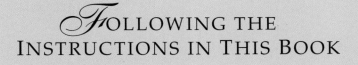

$\mathcal{F}$OLLOWING THE INSTRUCTIONS IN THIS BOOK

◆ All the step-by-step instructions for the designs are illustrated to make them easy to follow.

◆ Measurements are given to help you keep to the correct proportions – for example, the thickness of logs, the diameter of balls of clay and the lengths of cut pieces of log are given. Keep a ruler beside you as you work so that you can refer to it for accurate sizing.

◆ Precise quantities of clay needed to complete each project are not included but no design will require more than one 60gm (2oz) packet of clay.

2 · BEADS

Beads are one of the most ancient forms of jewellery, and they are found from the clay and wooden beads of early cultures through to the exotic plastics of today. Polymer modelling clays give the home craft worker the exciting opportunity to take part in this ancient craft and to produce glorious beads in all shapes, designs and colours. The following projects demonstrate a large range of different shapes and designs, but I hope you will use them as a starting point and be inspired to go on to produce your own patterns and designs.

Basic Bead-making Techniques

Bead-making in polymer clays is quite easy if you follow a few basic rules:

◆ Always try to make beads that are supposed to be the same size, *exactly* the same size. You can do this by rolling a log and cutting equal lengths for a set of beads. If you find it difficult to do this by eye, lie the log along a ruler and cut it at regular intervals.

◆ Once you have made a bead, handle it as little as possible before baking.

◆ Before baking, check that the holes in the beads are large enough to take your chosen thread, thong or wire. If you find that a hole is not large enough, it is possible to enlarge it by twisting a small bit from a power drill into the hole by hand.

◆ Choose mixtures of colours carefully. A few toning colours will often look far more successful than complicated combinations. Polymer clay colours are bright, so mix the clay for more subtle effects. In addition, vary the types and sizes of beads in one necklace. Modelling clay beads are hand-made, and slight irregularities are part of their charm. Putting different sizes and shapes together will look far more effective than if you try to mimic a string of perfectly symmetical, commercially made beads. However, if you combine your hand-made beads with commercial beads your designs will have more variety and you will be able to spend more time making a few beautiful feature beads rather than the dozens of small beads needed to make up a necklace. The most useful types of commercial beads are described on page 19.

◆ When you paint beads you will find that it is easier to paint tiny motifs with an artists' watercolour paintbrush than with a cheaper hobby brush, which has softer hair. Invest in a good number 0 brush and clean it thoroughly after use, because any acrylic paint left in the hairs will ruin it.

Basic Bead Types

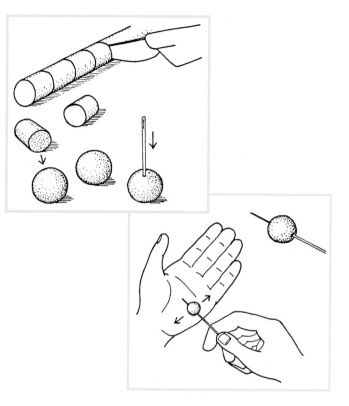

Round Beads

Roll a log of clay the same thickness as the diameter of the beads required. Cut lengths of the same measurement. Roll each length lightly between your palms, rotating your hands in a circular movement until the bead is quite round. Place it lightly on the board, then use a darning needle (or a pin for tiny beads) to pierce down-wards right through the centre of the bead. (See above left.)

Lift the bead on your needle and roll it back and forth against your palm to enlarge the hole and to correct the slight flattening caused by the piercing. Gently place the bead on the baking sheet, taking care to avoid touching it again before baking. There is no need to thread beads on to wires for baking. They will not distort on the baking sheet, and if you use baking parchment rather than foil, there should be no mark at all where they have rested on the parchment. It is possible to make beads very quickly with this technique. (See above right.)

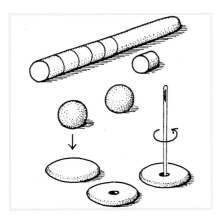

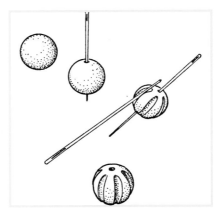

Disc Beads

Roll a log of clay and cut equal lengths to the size required. For example, a 6mm (¼in) thick log cut into 6mm (¼in) lengths will give disc beads 10mm (⅜in) in diameter. Roll the clay into balls between your hands and press each down on to the board with your finger until they are 10mm (⅜in) across. Use a blunt wool needle to pierce the centre of each, enlarging the hole with a circular motion. Slice the discs off the board with your craft knife and lift them on to the baking sheet.

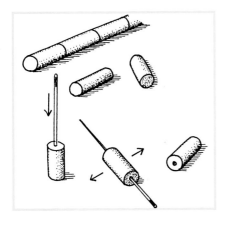

Tube Beads

These beads will be approximately the same size as the lengths of log cut. Stand each length upright on the board and pierce down through the centre with a darning needle. Holding the bead on the needle, roll it gently on the board to even out the sides. This will enlarge the hole and keep the bead round in cross-section.

Melon or Fluted Beads

First, make a round bead as above. When you have pierced the bead, hold it horizontally on the needle and press the side of a wool needle against it all round to indent the sides. Roll lightly against your palm to finish.

Pebble Beads

These beads, which resemble pebbles from the beach, show how versatile polymer clays can be. Pressing the clay with a piece of quilt wadding produces a wonderful texture, very similar to sandstone or granite. An added advantage is that they can be made with all the scraps of clay left over from other projects such as millefiori, as well as any squashed disasters!

Millefiori Beads

Millefiori means 'thousand flowers', and it is the name employed in glass-making to describe the use of coloured canes of glass that have a pattern running right through them, rather like seaside rock. Glass millefiori beads are made by applying slices of the canes to the sides of a bead to build up a pattern. A similar technique is possible with polymer modelling clay, and it can give extremely intricate results. Geometric patterns are the simplest designs to create, but it is also possible to build up complex images in a cane and reduce them to tiny detail by simply rolling or compressing the cane to reduce the diameter.

SPICE ISLAND NECKLACE AND EARRINGS SET

*T*his richly coloured set is made with a variety of the basic beads in toning colours and different sizes. It shows what sumptuous results can be achieved with polymer modelling clays. The purples and blues are mixed from different combinations of crimson, violet and blue to give a harmonious colour scheme, and the leaf green and gold are a perfect foil to the purples.

MATERIALS

For a 50cm (20in) necklace and earrings:

- ◆ Clay – violet, crimson, blue and leaf green
- ◆ Gold powder
- ◆ Beading thread
- ◆ GP torpedo clasp
- ◆ 2 GP calotte crimps
- ◆ 2 GP 4cm (1½in) headpins
- ◆ 2 GP fish-hook ear wires
- ◆ Gloss varnish

MIXTURES

- ◆ Plum = 1 violet + 1 crimson
- ◆ Royal blue = 1 violet + 1 blue
- ◆ Purple = 1 blue + 1 crimson

BEADS TO MAKE

- ◆ **Round beads**
  3 plum – 13mm (½in)
  2 plum – 10mm (⅜in)
  8 royal blue – 6mm (¼in)
  4 royal blue – 3mm (⅛in)
  36 purple – 3mm (⅛in)
- ◆ **Melon beads**
  4 gold – 10mm (⅜in)
- ◆ **Disc beads**
  16 gold – 6mm (¼in)
  6 leaf green – 6mm (¼in)
- ◆ **Tube beads**
  66 leaf green – 3mm (⅛in)

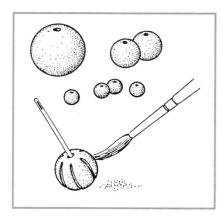

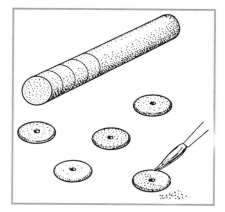

1 Make the round beads following the instructions for round beads on page 26. Make the melon beads using any colour clay and following the instructions on page 27 for melon beads. After indenting the sides, brush all over with gold powder, holding the bead steady by keeping the needle inside the hole as you brush.

2 The disc beads are made by rolling a 6mm (¼in) leaf green log and cutting 22 pieces, each 3mm (⅛in) long. Follow the instructions for disc beads on page 27. Brush 16 of the beads with gold powder, leaving the remaining six green.

3 The tube beads are quick and easy to make. Roll a 3mm (⅛ in) log and cut 66 3mm (⅛ in) lengths. Follow the instructions on page 27 for tube beads. Bake all the beads for 15 minutes. Varnish the gold, royal blue and plum beads, leaving the rest matt.

4 Make the earrings by threading each eyepin as follows: one purple 3mm (⅛ in) round bead, one gold disc bead, one plum 10mm (⅜ in) round bead, one gold disc, one royal blue 3mm (⅛ in) round bead, two tube beads, one 3mm (⅛ in) purple round bead. Turn a loop in the top of each headpin (see page 21). Attach the fish-hook ear wires.

5 String the beads for the necklace in the order shown in the figure, matching each side (see page 20 for stringing instructions). This makes the necklace approximately 50cm (20in) long, but you can make it shorter or longer by adding or subtracting small tube beads. Finish the necklace with calotte crimps and a clasp.

GRECIAN GOLD
NECKLACE

$\mathscr{B}$aked polymer clay has an excellent surface
that can be painted with acrylic paints.
The painted gold leaf design on these beads
was inspired by patterns on ancient
Greek pottery.

MATERIALS

- ◆ Clay – black
- ◆ Gold acrylic paint
- ◆ Nail varnish remover
- ◆ Gloss varnish
- ◆ 18 round GP beads 3 mm (⅛ in) diameter
- ◆ GP liquid gold beads
- ◆ 2 GP calotte crimps
- ◆ GP torpedo clasp
- ◆ Beading thread

BLACK BEADS TO MAKE

- ◆ 1 tube bead – 10 × 28 mm (⅜ × 1⅛ in)
- ◆ 2 round beads – 10 mm (⅜ in)
- ◆ 6 melon beads – 6 mm (¼ in)
- ◆ 2 disc beads – 10 mm (⅜ in)

1 Make the beads from black clay following the instructions on pages 26–27. When you have made the tube bead, curve it by pinching the two ends together at the top. This will cause the bead to hang with the curve downwards so that the painted side is always visible when it is worn. Bake the beads for 15 minutes.

2 Brush the tube bead and two round beads with nail varnish remover to de-grease them. Mark the outline of the design lightly with a pencil, then paint the design in gold acrylic paint, using the illustration above as a guide. Paint the wavy line first, then paint the leaves. It is easier to paint the round beads by holding them steady with a wool needle in the hole. Paint the melon beads and disc beads gold. Varnish the beads with gloss varnish when the gold paint is completely dry.

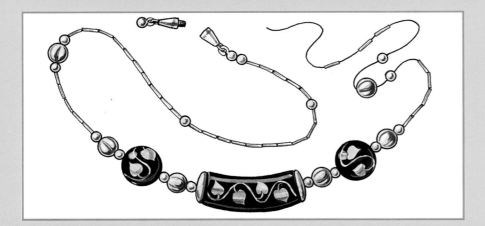

3 Thread the beads in the order shown (see left). The liquid gold beads are arranged in groups of fives and tens, and round metal beads are positioned between the groups and each clay bead. The disc beads are placed on either side of the central tube bead. Attach the calotte crimps and clasp (refer to page 20 for complete stringing instructions).

SANDSTONE THONG NECKLACE

$\mathcal{T}$his necklace uses pebble beads, which are described on page 27.

MATERIALS
- Clay – light brown, white, ochre, dark brown, yellow, orange, black and transparent
- Small piece of quilt wadding
- 1m (1yd) of 1mm (½2 in) natural leather thong

MIXTURE
- Beige = 1 light brown + 2 white

MARBLING
Marble together beige and combinations of two or three of the other colours in varying quantities (see marbling instructions on page 16). Form the marbled clay into logs, 10mm (⅜ in) thick.

1 Cut lengths of varying sizes, from the marbled logs. Take each length, roll it a little longer and fold in the cut edges. Make a rough ball shape and place it on the wadding, folding the top of the wadding over so that the clay is completely enclosed.

2 Texture the pebbles by pressing the clay inside the wadding into irregular shapes. The wadding will give the clay a granite-like texture. Remove the pebble from the wadding and use a large wool needle to make a hole that will accommodate a leather thong. Make about 15 beads in various marbled colours and include some plain beige ones. Bake for 10 minutes.

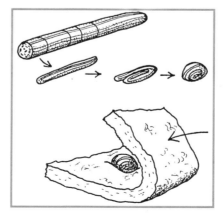

3 Thread the beads on to the thong as shown in step 2, tying a knot in the thong before and after each one. Arrange the single beads and groups of beads so that they are approximately 5cm (2in) apart. Allow plenty of thong length because the knots take it up. Finish the necklace with a knot. If you want a shorter necklace that will not pass over your head, you will need to attach a clasp (see page 21).

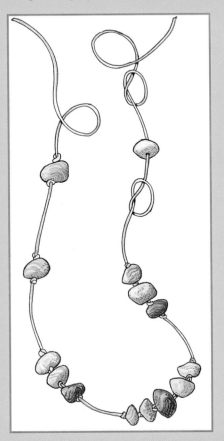

GRANITE CHOKER AND BRACELET

*T*his project also uses pebble beads, but this time for a choker and matching bracelet.

MATERIALS
- ◆ Clay – blue, grey, violet, green, white, black and transparent
- ◆ 1m (1yd) of 1mm (¹⁄₃₂in) black leather thong
- ◆ 4 SP spring ends
- ◆ 2 SP bolt rings or hooks

MIXTURES
Make the blue, violet and green clays more muted by mixing each with grey.

MARBLING
Marble the muted colours with white, grey, transparent and black (see page 16).

1 Follow the instructions for the Sandstone Thong Necklace on page 32 to make the pebble beads. Bake for 10 minutes.

2 Thread the beads on the black leather thong, with a knot on either side of the group. Trim the choker to 35cm (14in) and the bracelet to 18cm (7in) or to fit. Squeeze spring ends on to the ends of the thong and attach a clasp (see page 21 for instructions on finishing leather thong).

SPIDER'S WEB MILLEFIORI NECKLACE AND EARRINGS

*T*his eye-catching design is not difficult to make, but it needs patience. Try to keep your hands as cool as possible, particularly if you are working with soft clays. If things get sticky, rest the clay in the refrigerator for a while.

MATERIALS

- Clay – black, turquoise, violet, blue, golden-yellow and white
- Craft knife or razor blade
- SP 0.6mm wire
- 16 SP 3mm (⅛ in) round metal beads
- 6 SP 2.5cm (1in) eyepins
- 1 30cm (12in) SP chain with clasp
- 2 SP kidney wires

MIXTURES

Mix the turquoise, violet and blue clays with a little white to lighten them for greater contrast with the black.

BEADS TO MAKE

- Millefiori decorated black beads
  4 round beads – 10mm (⅜ in)
  1 tube bead – 20 × 6mm (¾ × ¼ in)
- Plain black beads
  8 round beads – 5mm (³⁄₁₆ in)

1 Roll out a sheet of black clay to about 1.5mm (¹⁄₁₆ in) thick and trim it to 2.5 × 7.5cm (1 × 3in). Form a 6mm (¼ in) log of the light turquoise clay, 7.5cm (3in) long, and lay it on the edge of the black clay sheet. Wrap the black around the turquoise and trim away the surplus. Roll the cane on the board until it is about 5mm (³⁄₁₆ in) thick. Repeat the process with the pale violet, blue and yellow clays.

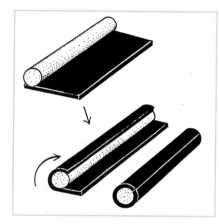

2 Cut the turquoise cane into four 7.5cm (3in) lengths and arrange them side-by-side on the board. Cut three similar lengths of violet cane and arrange them on top of the turquoise. Cut two lengths of pale blue cane and stack them on top, finishing with one length of yellow. Carefully press all the canes together to form a triangular cross-section.

3 Press the cane on the board all along its length, turning it to another side and repeating until it begins to lengthen. Hold it vertically in one hand and stroke it with the other, pulling it gently so that it elongates but keeps the triangular section. Press it on the board occasionally to keep it the same thickness along its length. Continue until the cane is 10mm (⅜in) thick and about 25cm (10in) long. Trim off the ends, which will be distorted.

4 Cut the cane into five equal lengths and arrange them so that all the yellow canes are in the centre and the different colours line up into concentric circles. Press the lengths together and roll on the board until the cane is 10mm (⅜in) thick. You are now ready to cut slices to decorate your beads.

5 Cut the cane in half to reveal the pattern in the centre because the pattern is likely to be distorted at the ends. Using a sharp new blade in your craft knife or a razor blade, cut slices about 1.5mm (¹⁄₁₆in) thick, rotating the cane by a quarter turn after cutting each slice to keep it round in shape.

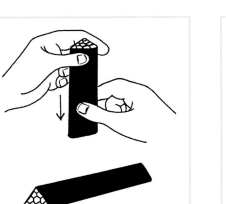

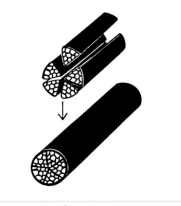

Other Ideas for Millefiori Canes

The photograph shows some other ways in which you can use millefiori slices and some different colour schemes. The disc pendant is made by flattening a ball of black clay into a disc 3cm (1¼in) across. Punch out the centre hole with the empty case of a ball-point pen. Apply millefiori slices and roll lightly to flatten them in. Bake and attach a leather thong.

The stud earrings and brooch are made by pressing slices of cane into milled cup fittings.

See page 116 for instructions on how to make buttons.

The hair clip is made in different colours, using white instead of black for wrapping the canes. Thread the beads onto a wire and twist the ends of the wire into the holes on a hair clip to secure.

6 Form four 10mm (⅜in) balls of black clay. Press four slices around the middle of each ball and one at each end, then gently roll the ball between your hands until the slices are smoothed in. They will distort slightly while you do this, but this adds to the design. Pierce the beads in the usual way, first with a pin and then with a thick wool needle to widen the hole.

7 To make the tube bead, cut about 12 slices of cane 1.5mm (¹⁄₁₆in) thick and arrange them in rows, fitting them together into a patchwork. Roll the surface of the slices lightly to flatten them into a smooth mat. Form a 6mm (¼in) log of black clay and cut a piece 20mm (¾in) long. Wrap the patchwork mat around this, folding the edges over the ends and trimming the surplus to fit exactly round.

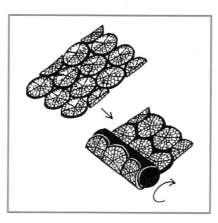

8 Roll the tube bead on the board to smooth it and press the ends down on the board to maintain the cylinder shape. Pierce a hole down the centre with the needle and then roll the sides of the bead on the board to enlarge the hole. Make eight 5mm (³⁄₁₆ in) plain round black beads. Bake the beads for 10 minutes. After baking varnish all the beads.

9 Cut two 11.5cm (4½ in) lengths of wire for the earrings. Turn a loop in one end of each and thread on the beads as shown below (see page 21 for instructions on loops). Turn a loop in the other end and bend the wire gently round in a circle, linking the two loops together. The natural curve of the wire should give a good circle. Attach a kidney wire to one of the linked loops on each earring. Alternatively, use ready-made ear hoops and thread the beads on to these.

10 Cut a 11.5cm (4½ in) length of wire for the necklace and turn a loop in one end. Thread the beads on to the wire in the order shown below and turn a loop in the other end of the wire. Turn loops in the ends of the eyepins and link them together, three each side, attaching them to the loops in the wire. Cut the chain in half by removing a central link and attach one end to each of the end eyepins.

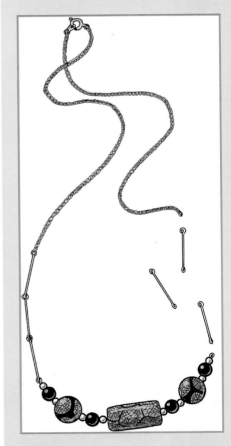

MILLEFIORI SUNFLOWER NECKLACE AND EARRINGS

Sunflowers are always popular flowers, and they combine beautifully with royal blue to make striking jewellery. This is a more advanced millefiori design, so if you have not attempted the technique before, try making the Spider's Web canes first.

MATERIALS

- ◆ Clay – yellow, golden-yellow, ochre, orange, leaf green, dark brown, blue and violet
- ◆ Craft knife or razor blade
- ◆ Yellow rocaille beads 2 or 3mm (⅛in)
- ◆ 2 small GP pendant mounts with top loops
- ◆ 4 GP jump rings
- ◆ 2 GP fish-hook ear wires
- ◆ Beading thread
- ◆ GP torpedo clasp
- ◆ 2 GP calotte crimps

MIXTURES

- ◆ Royal blue = 2 blue + 1 violet
- ◆ Pale leaf green = yellow + leaf green

BEADS TO MAKE

- ◆ Millefiori decorated beads
  5 round beads – 13mm (½in)
  6 round beads – 10mm (⅜in)
- ◆ Plain royal blue beads
  22 round beads – 6mm (¼in)
  36 round beads – 5mm (³⁄₁₆in)

For the earrings:

2 slices from the large cane – 3mm (⅛in) thick

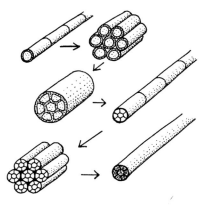

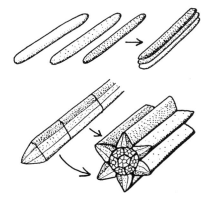

1 Form a 6mm (¼in) thick log of orange clay, 7.5cm (3in) long. Roll out a sheet of dark brown clay to 1.5mm (¹⁄₁₆ in) thick and trim to 2.5 × 7.5cm (1 × 3in). Wrap the orange log in the brown clay. Roll this cane to thin it to 3mm (⅛in) and cut seven equal lengths. Stack these together, six pieces around a central piece, and roll the new cane until it is about 10mm (⅜in) thick. Repeat the process once more and roll it to 6mm (¼in) thick. Cut a 5cm (2in) length of clay.

2 Form a 3mm (⅛in) thick log each of yellow, golden-yellow and ochre about 15cm (6in) long. Flatten each a little and stack one on top of the other, first the yellow, then the golden-yellow, then the ochre. Roll lightly to join them together, then press into a triangular cross-section along the length. Cut into six 5cm (2in) lengths and arrange these around the flower centre, keeping the points of the petals as sharply angled as possible.

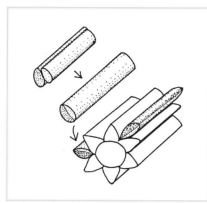

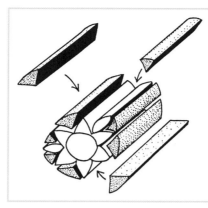

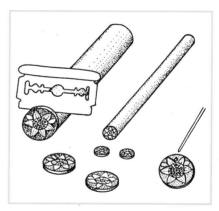

3 To make the leaves, roll a 3mm (⅛in) log each of leaf green and pale green, both 5cm (2in) long. Flatten them slightly and press together, rolling to form a cane.

4 Roll a long 6mm (¼in) log of royal blue clay and press it into a triangular cross-section.

Flatten the cane into a leaf-shaped cross-section and cut two 5cm (2in) lengths. Lay one length between two petals on one side of the flower and the other between two petals on the other side.

Cut the blue clay into 5cm (2in) lengths and then use these lengths to fill the gaps between the petals, rolling thinner lengths to pack in beside the leaf canes. Push the points well down between the petals and pack in some additional thin strips of clay as necessary so that the petals retain their shape.

5 Roll the cane until it is 10mm (⅜in) thick, cut it in half and roll one half to 3mm (⅛in) thick. Cut 1.5mm (¹⁄₁₆in) slices from both canes with a razor blade or sharp craft knife, giving the cane a quarter turn between each slice to minimize distortion. Cut two 3mm (⅛in) slices from the large cane for the earrings and make a hole in the top of each with a wool needle.

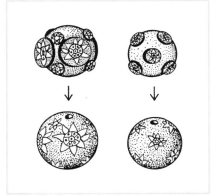

6 Make five 13mm (½in) balls of royal blue clay for the large beads and six 10mm (⅜in) balls for the medium beads. Apply four slices from the large cane around each of the large beads and then four small sunflower slices from the small cane to fill the spaces. Apply small sunflower slices evenly over the medium beads. Roll all the beads gently to smooth the sunflowers in and pierce in the usual way (see page 26).

7 Make 22 6mm (¼in) and 36 5mm (³⁄₁₆in) round royal blue beads. Bake all the beads and the earring slices for 10 minutes. Squeeze a pendant mount into the hole of each earring slice. Attach two jump rings to each mount and then a fish-hook ear wire. Using two jump rings makes the slices hang facing the front.

8 Thread the beads in the order shown above, placing a rocaille bead between each clay bead in the centre and between groups of three at the ends. The 6mm (¼ in) plain beads are positioned at the centre of the necklace with the 5mm (³⁄₁₆in) beads towards the ends. Attach calotte crimps and a clasp (see page 20 for stringing instructions).

Variations

Try giving the sunflowers eight petals instead of six by adding two more petal wedges. Some of the beads shown in the enlarged photograph opposite have eight-petalled flowers.

If you roll a sunflower cane to 3mm (⅛in) thick, it can be incorporated into the blue packing clay of another sunflower resulting in tiny flowers around the large sunflower.

FOSSIL BEAD NECKLACE

These beads are inspired by the fossils that are sometimes found in rocks on the seashore. The designs are stamped into the soft clay and then brushed with powder colour.

MATERIALS
- ◆ Clay – white, light brown and red
- ◆ Darning needle
- ◆ Several sea shells with varying textures
- ◆ Reddish-brown powder colour or artists' pastel
- ◆ Linen thread

MIXTURES
- ◆ Beige = 1 light brown + 2 white
- ◆ Terracotta = 1 red + 2 light brown

BEADS TO MAKE
- ◆ 9 large stamped beige beads
- ◆ 9 small stamped terracotta beads

1 To make the fish stamp, form a 5mm (³⁄₁₆ in) ball of scrap clay, shape into an oval and press it down on the board. Flatten a 3mm (⅛ in) ball of clay, trim it to a triangle for the tail and press it on the end of the body. Flatten a tiny log for the top fin, trim and press it on the fish. Mark an eye and a mouth and use the needle's eye to mark scales. Press a tiny oval on the bottom of the fish for a lower fin and mark lines on the fins and tail. Slice the fish off the board and bake for 10 minutes.

2 Make nine 13mm (½ in) balls of beige clay and shape them into ovals. Pierce one with the darning needle and, with the needle still in place, lay it on the board and press the fish stamp into the clay. With both the fish stamp and the needle still in place, turn over the bead and indent the back with a shell. Remove the fish stamp with the point of a needle and brush both impressions with reddish-brown powder colour. Remove the needle, twisting it to enlarge the hole to take the linen thread. Repeat with the other beads, varying the shells used.

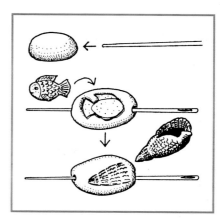

BEADS

42

3 Form the terracotta clay into nine 10mm (⅜in) balls. Pierce a ball with the darning needle and, with the needle still in place, press the clay onto the surface of a large shell to texture the underside.

Holding the bead on the large shell with the needle, use the point of a shell to make a star pattern on the other side. Twist the bead a few times to enlarge the hole and remove the needle. Repeat with the other teracotta beads. Bake all the beads for 10 minutes.

4 When the beads are cool, string them on the linen thread, tying a knot before and after each bead and spacing them about 4cm (1½in) apart.

Tie a knot in the thread to finish. If the thread is difficult to pass through the holes, stiffen the end with glue.

Black and Gold Fossil Necklace
The black and gold version is made using only black clay and by brushing the fish stamp and the shells with gold powder before making each impression. After baking, varnish the gold powder and link the beads with eyepins (see page 21 for instructions on linking eyepins). Arrange six large and five small beads alternately and attach a gold plated chain to the ends.

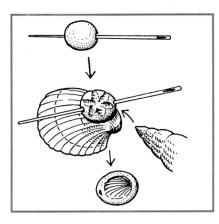

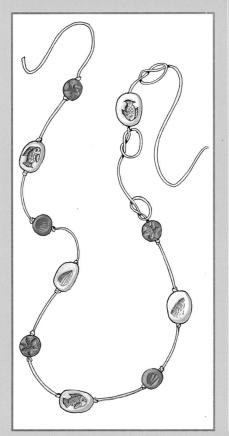

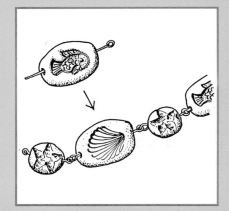

3 ·  FLOWERS AND FRUIT

Polymer clays can be used to imitate flowers, leaves and fruit, and the results make some quite delectable jewellery. It is also possible to work to an extremely small scale because of the fine quality of the clays, so stud earrings or rings of tiny flowers can be given minute details. Stud or clip earrings and rings are worked flat on the board and glued to the findings after baking. A longer baking time should make them reasonably robust, but they still need to be treated with care because levering against the clay when, for example, removing an earring could break it. Dangling earrings, which are subject to far less wear, can be made more fanciful and delicate.

HAREBELL DANGLERS

*T*hese pretty earrings use artificial stamens of the kind that can be purchased from cake decorating or craft shops. Try making the harebells in other pastel colours, such as lilac or yellow.

MATERIALS

- Clay – transparent and blue mixed to make pastel blue
- Talcum powder
- Small paintbrush handle or similar blunt tool
- Yellow artificial flower stamens
- 2 SP 2.5cm (1 in) eyepins
- Superglue
- 2 SP kidney wires

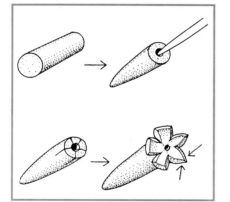

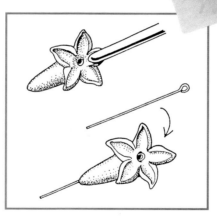

1 Roll a log of pastel blue clay 6mm (¼ in) thick and cut two pieces 13mm (½ in) long. Thin one end of each into a point. Make a hole in the broad end of each about 6mm (¼ in) deep and 3mm (⅛ in) wide. Insert the knife into this hole and make five cuts all round. Splay out the cut pieces and pinch each into a point.

2 Dust your fingers with talcum powder and press each petal outwards against your finger with the end of a paintbrush handle to thin and cup it. Curve the petals up a little. Thread an eyepin through the centre of each flower until the loop is slightly embedded in the clay. Bake the flowers, standing upright on their petals, for about 10 minutes.

3 When cool, trim four stamens to about 20mm (¾ in) long, varying their lengths a little. Glue these into the centre of the flower, pushing them down into the hole beside the eyepin. Trim the eyepin where it protrudes and turn a loop in the end (see page 21). Attach the kidney wires.

FUCHSIA DANGLERS

These striking earrings can be made in a variety of fuchsia colours – pink and white, pale pink and cream, or white and lilac.

Outlines for the fuchsia

MATERIALS

- Clay – transparent, crimson and violet
- Tracing paper and pencil
- Small teaspoon or blunt modelling tool
- Talcum powder
- 4 SP 2.5cm (1in) headpins; trim two to 20mm (¾in)
- 4 rocaille beads, transparent or pearly
- 2 SP 2.5cm (1in) eyepins
- 2 SP kidney wires
- Jam jar
- Wire

MIXTURES

- Purple = 1 violet + 2 transparent
- Pink = 1 crimson + 2 transparent

1 Trace the two outlines and cut them out. Roll out two 13mm (½in) balls of purple clay to about 1mm (¹⁄₃₂in) thick. Lay on the petal outline and use your knife to cut out two sets of petals. Repeat with the pink clay and the calyx outline. Slice carefully under each cut-out piece to free it from the board. Dust your fingers with talc to prevent sticking and use a small teaspoon or modelling tool to press each petal against your fingers to cup it, thinning the edges as you work.

2 Thread a bead on to each headpin and turn a loop in the top, attaching one of each length on to an eyepin (see page 21). Form a 6mm (¼in) ball of purple and cut in half. Thread each eyepin through a half ball of clay until the loop is against the cut edge. Thread the petals on to the eyepin, pushing them down on to the half ball so they hang down all round. Mark faint vertical lines on the outsides of the petals with the knife blade. Repeat with the calyx and tip the points up slightly.

3 Stretch a piece of wire across the top of a jam jar. Carefully turn a loop in the top of each eyepin and suspend the flowers from the wire so that they do not distort during baking. Bake for 10 minutes. When cool, attach a kidney wire to each earring.

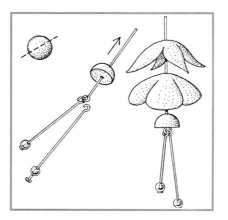

LILY-OF-THE-VALLEY BROOCH

*T*his delicate brooch uses beading wire for the flower stems and transparent clay to give the flowers a realistic translucence. Try making several to twist together to decorate a straw hat.

MATERIALS
- ◆ Clay – transparent, leaf green and yellow
- ◆ Talcum powder
- ◆ Small paintbrush handle or similar blunt tool
- ◆ GP or brass beading wire
- ◆ Leaves with straight veins (lily or montbretia are ideal)
- ◆ Brooch back
- ◆ Glue

MIXTURE
- ◆ Translucent yellow = transparent + yellow

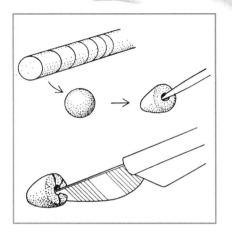

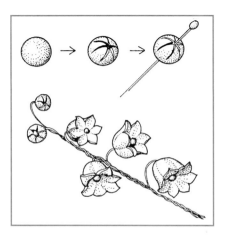

1 Roll a 6mm (¼in) log of transparent clay and cut six lengths, ranging from 3mm (⅛in) to 1.5mm (¹⁄₁₆in) long. Starting with the largest piece, form a ball, then a cone, and make a hole in one side with a wool needle, opening it out by twisting the needle. Insert the tip of the knife into the hole and make six cuts. Separate the petals and pinch each one into a point.

2 Dust your fingers with talcum powder and press each petal against your finger with a small paintbrush handle to thin and cup it. Cut a 5cm (2in) length of beading wire and turn a loop at one end. Press a tiny ball of translucent yellow on to the loop and thread the other end of the wire into the centre of the flower, pulling it through until the yellow ball is inside the flower. Curve the petals out. Repeat with three other flowers.

3 Form the two smallest lengths of clay into balls for the buds. Make three cuts halfway through each ball and fix a tiny yellow ball on a wire as for the flowers, pulling it inside the larger bud. The smaller bud has just a wire loop pulled inside. Bake the flowers for 10 minutes. Arrange the flowers, buds at the top, in order of size and twist the wires together. Trim to 6.5cm (2½in) from top bud to bottom of stem.

SWEET VIOLETS HAIR CLIP

'Recluse and sweet', said Christina Rossetti of these dainty flowers, harbingers of spring, and what nicer way is there to wear flowers than in your hair?

MATERIALS

- ◆ Clay – transparent, violet, yellow and leaf green
- ◆ Well-veined leaves
- ◆ 7.5cm (3in) hair clip or barrette
- ◆ Glue

MIXTURES

Mix transparent with both the violet and yellow for a translucent look

1 Follow the instructions on page 52 for making rose leaves, using the rose leaf outline or a cutter. Arrange the leaves on the hair clip, overlapping them as shown. Roll a 6mm (¼in) log of the violet mixture and cut 15 slices 1.5mm (¹⁄₁₆in) thick. Form these into tear drop shapes and press down onto the board to make petals. Mark faint vertical lines with the knife blade. Arrange petals as shown below for the first two flowers.

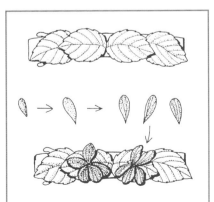

2 Arrange a further flower in the centre and make a hole in the centre of each flower. Press a tiny ball of yellow into the hole. Form a 3mm (⅛in) ball of leaf green for the bud calyx and point both ends, make two cuts into one end and fold it around a small oval of violet clay. Insert the bud under the leaves. Add two more made-up buds. Bake the clay on the hair clip for 20 minutes. When cool, glue it to the clip, leaving a section of metal showing so that you will not have to press against the clay to open and close the clip.

4 Make the leaves from two 13mm (½in) balls of leaf green. Point one end of each and press on the board, flattening each into a leaf shape 3mm (⅛in) thick in the middle and thinner at the edges. Use a real leaf to impress vertical veins on the clay leaves. Overlap the two leaves as shown above, lay the flowers in the centre and curve the base of the leaves round the flower stem, squeezing the clay to secure them. Bake for 15 minutes. Glue on a brooch back and bend the flowers to droop slightly.

DAISY CHAIN NECKLACE

*T*his dainty necklace is a combination of polymer clay flowers and leaves with tiny glass rocailles and bugles.

FLOWERS AND FRUIT

50

MATERIALS

- Clay – transparent, yellow, orange and leaf green
- Talcum powder
- Paintbrush handle or similar blunt tool
- Glass beads – pearly white bugles 8mm (5/16 in) long; pearly lemon 1.5mm (1/16 in) rocailles
- Bead thread

MIXTURES

- Pastel orange = 1 orange + 2 transparent
- Pastel yellow = 1 yellow + 2 transparent
- Pastel green = 1 leaf green + 2 transparent

BEADS TO MAKE

- 5 pastel orange flowers
- 8 pastel yellow flowers
- 5 transparent flowers
- 8 leaves

1 For each daisy, form a 6mm (1/4 in) ball of clay and press it down on the board until it is 10mm (3/8 in) across. Cut out five V-shaped notches evenly around the edge. Slice off the board and pinch each petal into a rounded shape. Smear talc on your fingers and press each petal against your finger with a blunt tool to cup it. Indent the centre of the flower and make a hole right through for threading.

2 Roll a 6mm (1/4 in) log of the pastel green mixture and cut eight 3mm (1/8 in) lengths. Roll each into an oval and make a point at one end. Press down on the board but leave the blunt end unflattened. Mark veins with the knife and slice off the board, turn over and mark veins on the back. Pinch the blunt end and pierce it horizontally with a needle. Give the leaf a twist and lay on a baking sheet.

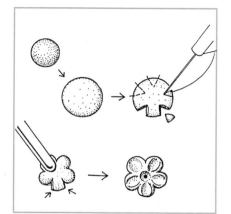

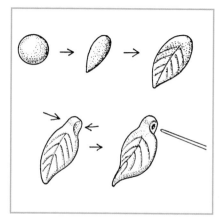

ROSE CORSAGE

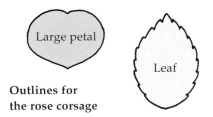

*T*hese delicate corsages borrow sugar paste techniques from cake decorating. It is possible to buy special cutters for making a wide variety of sugar paste flowers from specialist cake decorating shops, and these work very well with polymer modelling clay. Try to keep your hands as cool as possible to prevent the clay from going sticky. If necessary, cool the clay in a refrigerator for a while.

3 Bake the flowers and leaves for 15 minutes. When cool, string in the order shown below, using a round rocaille in the centre of each flower and spacing them with two or three bugles alternating with rocailles. Vary the spacing to give a more natural look (see page 20 for stringing instructions).
No clasp is needed, so knot the thread and take the ends back through the first few beads.

MATERIALS

◆ Clay – transparent and leaf green.
◆ Fine, green-coated florists' wire
◆ Sugar paste cutters for a small rose leaf and calyx or tracing paper and pencil
◆ Small paintbrush handle or similar blunt tool
◆ Crimson powder colour or artists' pastel
◆ Rose leaves or any well-veined leaf
◆ Talcum powder
◆ Dressmaker's pins
◆ Jam jar
◆ Florists' green tape
◆ Brooch back or safety pin

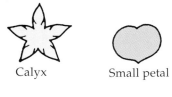

Calyx   Small petal

Large petal

Leaf

**Outlines for
the rose corsage**

1 Cut a 10cm (4in) length of florists' wire and turn the top into a small hook. Squeeze a 3mm (⅛in) ball of transparent clay onto the hook. Make two 3mm (⅛in) balls of transparent clay and roll them flat into ovals approximately 13mm (½in) across. Push a small dent in the top. Wrap the first petal around the clay ball on the wire and add the second petal slightly more loosely, turning the tops out a little.

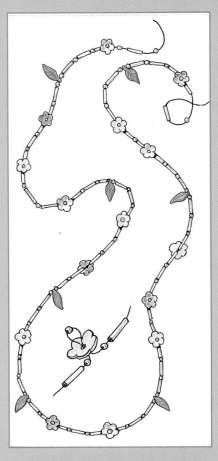

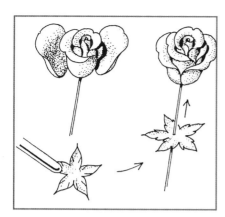

2 Make three 5mm (³⁄₁₆ in) balls of transparent clay and roll them into large petals, using the petal outline as a guide. Wrap these around the smaller petals, making each consecutive petal more open and turning the top edge outwards. Roll flat some leaf green clay 1.5mm (¹⁄₁₆ in) thick and trace the calyx outline or use a cutter to make a calyx. Thin and cup the sections by pressing with a blunt tool. Thread on to the wire and push up to the base of the rose.

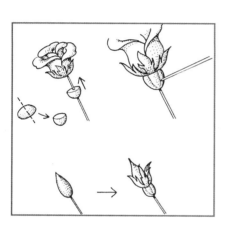

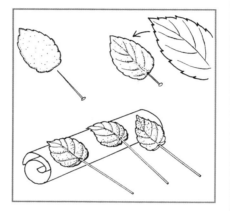

3 Form a 6mm (¼ in) ball of leaf green clay and cut it in half for a hip. Thread it on to the wire, pushing it up against the base of the rose. Mark lines down the hip. Make a second rose in the same way. Make a large bud using only three of the smaller petals. The small bud is a 6mm (¼ in) ball of transparent clay, pointed at one end, with the calyx wrapped round it and a smaller hip. Lightly brush the petal edges with crimson powder colour.

4 Roll out leaf green clay to 1.5mm (¹⁄₁₆ in) thick and cut out three leaves, using the outline or a rose leaf cutter. Pierce the base of each leaf with a pin and leave the pins in place. Impress veins onto the clay leaf with the underside of a real leaf. Replace the pins with 10cm (4in) lengths of wire and lay the leaves over a roll of paper to curve them while they bake.

5 Stretch a piece of wire across the top of a jam jar, make a hook in the end of each rose's wire and hang them in the jam jar for baking. Bake for 15 minutes. Tape the roses and leaves together into a spray using florists' tape. Trim the ends of the wires and wind the tape back on itself to finish. Angle the flowers and leaves into an attractive shape and tape on a safety pin or brooch back.

MATERIALS

- Clay – blue, violet, yellow, transparent and leaf green
- 5mm (³/₁₆ in) flat pad stud earrings or clips
- SP 0.8mm wire for the rings
- Glue
- Large marker pen, with a barrel of about 20mm (¾ in), or a similar cylindrical object for shaping the rings

MIXTURES

- Mix three different shades of blue by combining varying small quantities of blue and violet
- Mix transparent with all the shades, including the yellow, to give translucent colours

FORGET-ME-NOT EARRINGS AND RINGS

*T*hese are made almost entirely with a craft knife because your fingers will be too large! Forget-me-nots come in various shades of blue, and you can put several blues together in each cluster.

1 To make the earrings, form two 3mm (⅛ in) balls of leaf green clay and press them on to the board for the bases. Roll a log just under 3mm (⅛ in) thick of one of the blue mixtures and cut a thin slice for the first petal. Lift this on your knife, turn the knife over and press the petal down on the bottom corner of one of the bases. Continue round the flower, until there are five overlapping petals on each pad.

2 Make the second two flowers in the same way, using another shade of blue and positioning them above the first. Make the third flower, using a third shade of blue. Roll a 1mm (¹/₃₂ in) log of translucent yellow and cut tiny slices for the centres. Pierce each centre with a wool needle. Carefully slice them off the board and bake for about 10 minutes. When cool, glue the bases to the flat pads of the ear studs (see page 22 for gluing instructions).

3 To make a ring, cut a length of wire 13mm (½ in) long and turn a loop in each end (see page 21). Press a 3mm (⅛ in) ball of leaf green clay flat on the board, lay the wire across it and press another 3mm (⅛ in) ball on top, trapping the wire. Apply three forget-me-nots as for the earrings. Bake for 10 minutes. Curve a piece of wire around a pen to shape it. Cut the wire to fit your finger, allowing a 3mm (⅛ in) overlap. Turn a loop at one end, try for size and trim if necessary before turning the second loop. Attach to the loops on the forget-me-nots.

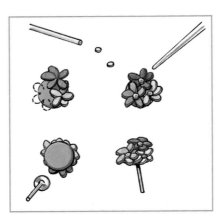

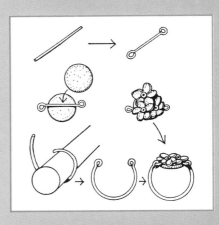

PEACH EARRINGS

*L*uscious peaches are made realistic by a dusting of powder colour. Alternatively, they can be made with red clay and varnished to make delightful cherry earrings.

MATERIALS

- ◆ Clay – transparent, yellow and leaf green
- ◆ 4 GP 4cm (1½in) headpins
- ◆ Crimson powder colour or artists' pastel
- ◆ 2 GP peg and loop fittings
- ◆ 2 GP French ear wires

MIXTURES

- ◆ Translucent yellow = 2 transparent + 1 yellow

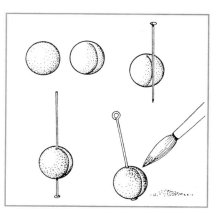

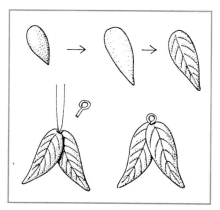

1 Form four 10mm (⅜in) balls of translucent yellow for the peaches. Press a pin into the side of each ball to indent it. Trim two of the headpins to 30mm (1¼in) long. Pierce each ball with a headpin as shown above, pushing it down onto the head of the pin, and turn a loop in the top of each (see page 21). Brush crimson powder colour on to the sides of the peaches to give a rosy blush.

2 Roll a 6mm (¼in) log of leaf green and cut four 3mm (⅛in) lengths. Form into ovals, point one end and press into leaf shapes on the board. Mark veins and lightly press together in pairs, curving the leaf points outwards. Make a hole in the top of each pair with a needle and insert a peg and loop fitting.

BLACKBERRY EARRINGS

*B*lackberries are one of nature's most delightful designs – dark reds and purples perfectly complement green foliage, and the spiky leaves are a wonderful contrast to the round, shiny berries.

MATERIALS
- ◆ Clay – violet, crimson, blue and leaf green
- ◆ 2 SP 4cm (1½in) headpins
- ◆ 2 SP kidney wires
- ◆ Gloss varnish

MIXTURES
- ◆ Purple = 1 blue + 1 crimson
- ◆ Plum = 1 violet + 1 crimson

1 Form two 10mm (⅜in) balls of purple clay and pierce to make round beads (see page 26). From purple and plum clay make lots of tiny balls about 3mm (⅛in) diameter and some a little smaller. Press these lightly over the beads to cover the surface completely, taking care to keep the hole open. Form two 6mm (¼in) balls of leaf green, point one end of each and press on to the board into a leaf shape 1.5mm (¹⁄₁₆in) thick. Mark veins, cut a zig-zag edge and apply a tiny stalk.

2 Thread the berries on to the headpins. Press the leaves on top, curving them round the headpins as shown below. Bake for 10 minutes. Varnish the berries, leaving the leaves matt. Turn a loop in the top of each headpin and attach the kidney wires (see page 21)

3 Bake all the pieces for 10 minutes. When cool, turn loops in the top of each peach's headpin. Remove the peg and loop fittings from the leaves and glue them back in firmly. Open the loops of the ear wires and thread on the leaves, the shorter peach, and lastly, the longer peach. Squeeze the loops shut.

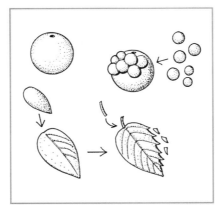

4 · ANIMAL JEWELLERY

Polymer clay is ideal for making charming animal jewellery because the rounded forms of animal bodies lend themselves to reproduction in soft clay. Animals have been popular in jewellery from the beginning of time and reached an especially high level of design during the early Middle Ages in Europe, when exotic zoomorphic jewellery echoed the stunningly beautiful artwork found in illuminated manuscripts of the time. Many cultures from all over the world have used animals as motifs in jewellery – from the eagles of the ancient Egyptians to the dragonflies of Art Nouveau, animals continued to inspire the craft jeweller.

The designs in this chapter can easily be adapted for different types of jewellery. For example, the basic penguin design could be made into a hair clip or a pendant, while the rabbit ear studs could be enlarged and made into dangling earrings. Try creating your own animal designs; illustrations in children's books are a useful source of ideas.

PIG BROOCH AND EAR STUDS

MATERIALS
- ◆ Clay – red, white and black
- ◆ Gloss varnish
- ◆ Brooch back
- ◆ 2 GP or SP flat pad ear studs or clips
- ◆ Glue

MIXTURE
- ◆ Pig pink = 1 red + 8 white

*T*here is something inexplicably appealing about a fat little pig with an expectant expression. These instructions make earrings 6mm (¼ in) across. If you find this too tiny, double the cut lengths of log to make earrings 13mm (½ in) across.

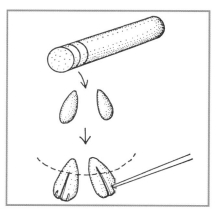

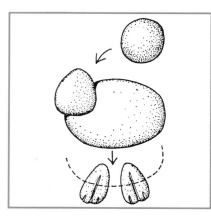

1 To make the brooch, roll a pink log 6mm (¼ in) thick and cut two pieces 3mm (⅛ in) long for the legs of the pig. Form these into oval shapes and press them on to the board, so that they splay out slightly, about 3mm (⅛ in) apart. Mark the centre of each to make it look like two legs, and then make a small indentation at the bottom of each leg to represent trotters.

2 Form a 13mm (½ in) ball of pink for the body, make it into an egg shape and press down on the board, covering the tops of the legs. Form a 10mm (⅜ in) ball for the head and press it on the top of the body at one end, nipping the top a little to shape the head.

3 Form two 3mm (⅛ in) balls for ears and point the top of each. Press on to the top of the head and poke an ear hole with a wool needle, pressing down against the head to secure. Cut a 1.5mm (¹⁄₁₆ in) slice from a 3mm (⅛ in) log for the snout and position onto the front of the head. Make two nostrils with the needle.

4 Make two eye-sockets with a pointed tool and fill them with two tiny black balls for the eyes. Form a 3mm (⅛ in) ball of pink and roll into a thin tail. Fix it to the rear of the body at one end, curling it round and pressing lightly to secure. Bake the pig for 10 minutes and, when cool, varnish the eyes and glue on a brooch back.

5 Work on both earrings at the same time so that they match. From a 3mm (⅛ in) thick log of pink clay cut four slices about 1mm (¹⁄₃₂ in) thick for the legs. Form these into ovals and press onto the board in two pairs. Mark lines and trotters as for the brooch (see step 1). Cut two 6mm (¼ in) lengths for the bodies, form into ovals and press over the tops of the legs. Cut two 3mm (⅛ in) lengths for the heads, roll into balls and press on to the bodies, on opposite sides to make a matching pair.

6 From a 1mm (¹⁄₃₂ in) log of pink clay cut two thin slices for snouts and lift them into place with the tip of your knife. Pierce two nostrils in each with a pin. Cut four slices, 1.5mm (¹⁄₁₆ in) thick, for ears and apply as for the brooch pig's ears. Roll two tiny tails and twirl into a curl on each rump. Poke eyes with a pin. Bake for 10 minutes and when cool, glue to the ear studs (see page 22 for gluing instructions).

PARROT BROOCH

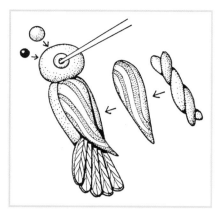

*T*his brightly coloured bird can be made in various colour schemes – try turquoise and yellow feathers for a blue and gold macaw. Feathers are textured on the parrot's wing using a wool needle or knife.

MATERIALS

- ◆ Clay – red, blue, green, yellow, orange and black
- ◆ Gloss varnish
- ◆ Brooch back
- ◆ Glue

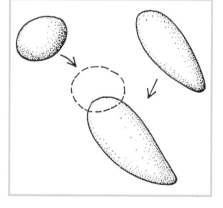

1 Form a 13mm (½ in) ball of red clay for the body. Shape it into an oval, point one end and press it down on to the board, curving the breast out a little. Form a 10mm (⅜ in) ball of red for the head and press on to the top of the body.

2 To make tail feathers, form a log of blue clay 10mm (⅜ in) thick and press it on to the board until it is about 5mm (³⁄₁₆ in) thick. Cut two slices, 1.5mm (¹⁄₁₆ in) thick, for feathers and lift each on to the bottom of the body with the knife. Make two yellow feathers and one green feather and fan them out as shown above. Mark feathering with the knife.

3 Marble lightly together blue and green clays, form into a log 6mm (¼ in) thick and cut a 20mm (¾ in) length. Shape into an oval and thin one end. Flatten on to the body for the wing, curving the pointed end over the top of the tail feathers. Make a 3mm (⅛ in) ball of yellow clay and press on to the head. Poke an eye socket in the centre. Make a small ball of black clay, 1.5mm (¹⁄₁₆ in) in diameter, and press lightly into the eye socket.

4 Form a ball of black clay, 6mm (¼in) in diameter, for the beak and point one end until it is 13mm (½in) long. Press the wide end on to the head and indent two nostrils with the wool needle to secure. Curve the beak down under the chin. Form a small oval of orange for the foot and press on underneath the body with the side of the wool needle. Mark feathers on the top of the wing with the eye of the needle. Bake for 10 minutes and, when cool, varnish the parrot's eye and glue on a brooch back (see page 22 for gluing instructions).

SIAMESE CAT HAIR CLIP

*C*ats are always favourite subjects for jewellery, and this row of snuggled together felines makes an unusual and appealing hair clip. Make all the cats at the same time so that they match.

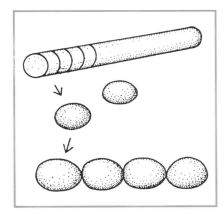

MATERIALS

- ◆ Clay – dark brown, white, blue and black
- ◆ 7.5cm (3 in) hair clip
- ◆ Small paintbrush handle or similar blunt tool
- ◆ Glue
- ◆ Gloss varnish

MIXTURES

- ◆ Beige = white + small quantity brown clay
- ◆ Pale blue = white + small quantity blue clay

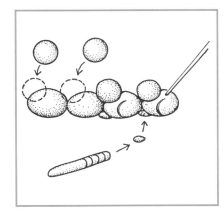

1 Form a 6mm (¼in) log of beige and cut four 15mm (⅝in) lengths for the cat bodies and four more lengths of 10mm (⅜in) for the heads. Form the body pieces into ovals and press them on to the board in a line, so that each just touches the one next to it. The resulting row should be just shorter than the hair clip.

2 Form the head pieces into balls and press them on to the left-hand side of the bodies. They should slightly overlap the rear of the cat in front. Roll a 3mm (⅛in) log of dark brown and cut four 3mm (⅛in) lengths for the front paws. Shape these into ovals and press on under the bodies. Mark claws with a knife. Mark the curve of the back legs with the point of a wool needle.

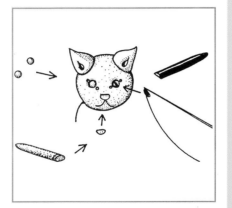

3 Cut eight pieces 3mm (⅛ in) long from a 3mm (⅛ in) log of dark brown for the ears. Form into balls, point one end of each and position on top of the heads, poking an ear hole with the wool needle and pressing down to secure. Pinch the ears into points. Indent two eye sockets in each head with your pointed tool and make a small indentation on either side of each socket with a wool needle to slant the eyes.

Variations

The black cat hair clip is made in the same way as the Siamese cat hair clip but using black clay for the bodies and yellow for the eyes. The eyes can be made more startling by forming them into ovals before pressing them on to the heads. Try marking whiskers on the cats' faces.

These are just two possible colour schemes, but you could make them in any colour you choose. Try marbling together grey and white clays for a group of tabbies.

4 Form eight tiny balls of equal size in pale blue to fit in the eye sockets. Roll a thin log of black 1.5mm (1/16 in) thick and lightly flatten. Cut thin slices of this and lift carefully into position on the eyes with the point of the knife to create pupils. Roll a log of dark brown 1.5mm (1/16 in) thick and cut slices for the noses, positioning them on to the fronts of the faces with the knife. Mark lines under the noses for mouths.

5 Cut four 20mm (¾ in) lengths from the dark brown 3mm (⅛ in) log for the tails. Form into tails, with one end pointed and the other blunt. Curve round the bodies as shown above, curling the tips over the front paws. Carefully slice under the cats with your knife and lift the whole piece on to the hair clip. Bake the cats on the hair clip for 15 minutes and allow to cool. Glue to the hair clip (see page 49), and paint the eyes with a gloss varnish.

FROG EAR STUDS

Tiny frogs, crouching on a pebble, make amusing studs that appeal to the young and the young at heart alike. If you prefer, make them twice as big by doubling the lengths in the instructions. Make both earrings at the same time so that they match.

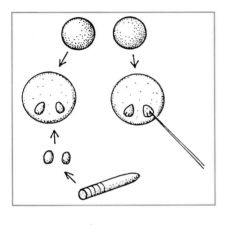

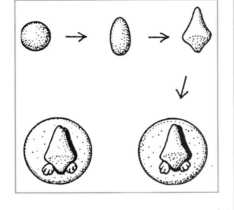

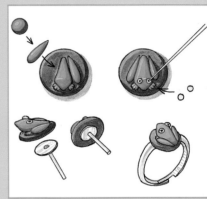

1 Form two balls of dark brown clay 5mm (³⁄₁₆ in) in diameter and press them down on the board until they are discs 8mm (⁵⁄₁₆ in) across. Roll a 1.5mm (¹⁄₁₆ in) log of green and cut four 1mm (¹⁄₃₂ in) lengths for the feet. Form these into tiny ovals and press down on the discs. Mark toes with the point of a pin.

2 Form two 3mm (⅛ in) balls of green for the bodies. Roll into ovals and pinch into the appropriate shape with your thumb and forefinger. Press the bodies down over the front feet.

3 Cut four 1.5mm (¹⁄₁₆ in) slices from a 3mm (⅛ in) thick green log for the back legs and roll into ovals, thinning one end of each slightly. Press these on either side of the bodies, the thin end to the back. Make four tiny balls of yellow for eyes and press on the front of the heads. Make a hole in the centre of each with the pin. Bake for 10 minutes and, when cool, glue to the ear studs (see page 22).

Frog Rings
The same design can be used to make a ring. Glue the frog to the pad of a flat pad ring finding. Tropical frogs come in a wonderful rainbow of colours, so you do not have to use green.

63

WHITE RABBIT EAR STUDS

*P*early white with a touch of pink, these little earrings go with most colour schemes and only reveal themselves as tiny rabbits from close by, which adds to their charm. Make both earrings at the same time so that they match.

MATERIALS

◆ Clay – white, pink and black
◆ 5mm (³⁄₁₆ in) flat pad ear studs or clips
◆ Glue

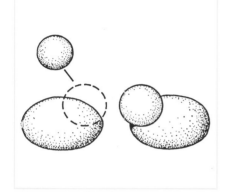

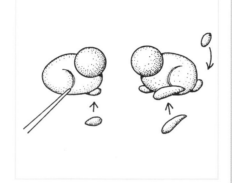

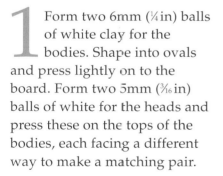

1 Form two 6mm (¼ in) balls of white clay for the bodies. Shape into ovals and press lightly on to the board. Form two 5mm (³⁄₁₆ in) balls of white for the heads and press these on the tops of the bodies, each facing a different way to make a matching pair.

2 Make two 1.5mm (¹⁄₁₆ in) balls and press under the front of each body for front paws. Mark the back leg curve with the tip of a wool needle. Form a 3mm (⅛ in) thick log of white and cut two 1.5mm (¹⁄₁₆ in) lengths for back legs, shape into long ovals and press on. Press on small balls of white for the tails.

3 Cut four 1.5mm (¹⁄₁₆ in) lengths from a 3mm (⅛ in) white log and shape into ears with one pointed end. Place two on each head as shown above, lying along the rabbit's back. Form two 1.5mm (¹⁄₁₆ in) balls of pink into ear shapes and press on to the middle of each lower ear. Indent these with the side of the wool needle. Pat on a tiny slice of pink for each nose. Make eye sockets with the wool needle and fill each with a tiny ball of black. Bake the rabbits for 10 minutes and, when cool, glue on to the ear stud pads (see page 22 for gluing instructions).

OWL EARRINGS AND PENDANT

*O*wls have a wonderful warm brown colouring, and this is reflected in the colours of the clay used in these designs. Try experimenting with other colours, such as creams and light browns, to make a barn owl. Work on both earrings at the same time so that they look the same.

MATERIALS

- ◆ Clay – dark brown, ochre, black, orange and white
- ◆ 2 SP 2.5cm (1 in) eyepins
- ◆ 2 SP kidney wires
- ◆ 1 SP triangular bail
- ◆ 1 SP chain
- ◆ 1 SP jump ring

1 To make the earrings, secure the eyepins as for step 1 of the penguin earrings (see page 66). Form two 3mm (⅛ in) balls of dark brown for the tails, point one end of each and press it flat on the board, just below the secured eyepins. Form two 6mm (¼ in) balls of ochre clay, shape them into ovals and press on to the embedded eyepins and tops of the tails. Mark the breasts with the eye of a wool needle to represent feathers and make vertical lines on the tails.

2 Cut four 6 mm (¼ in) lengths from a 3mm (⅛ in) dark brown log for wings, roll them into ovals and point one end of each. Flatten each into a wing shape and press on the tops of the bodies. Mark feathers on the wings with the eye of a wool needle. Form two 6mm (¼ in) brown balls for the heads and press on to the tops of the bodies.

3 Roll a black log, a little less than 3mm (⅛ in) thick, and cut two 10mm (⅜ in) lengths for the perches. Roll a 1.5mm (¹⁄₁₆ in) log of orange clay and cut four 3mm (⅛ in) lengths for the feet. Thin one end of each foot and press on the board so they make little triangles. Make two cuts in the wide end of each, splay out the toes and curve round the perches. Press the perches, with the feet attached, on to the bottom of the bodies.

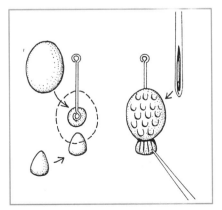

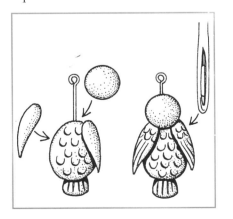

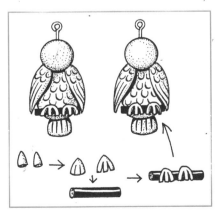

4 Form four 1.5mm (¹⁄₁₆ in) balls of white for eyes and press these flat on to the heads. Poke a hole in the centre of each eye with a wool needle and place a tiny ball of black in each. Roll a 1.5mm (¹⁄₁₆ in) log of brown and cut four 3mm (⅛ in) lengths for the 'ears'. Shape into ovals with one end pointed and press lightly on to the face above the eyes, curving the points upwards.

5 Roll a tiny log of orange clay, pointed at each end and cut off the points for beaks, lifting each into place with the knife. Make two small dents for nostrils to secure. Bake for 10 minutes and, when cool, attach the kidney wires to the eyepins (see page 21).

PENGUIN EARRINGS AND BROOCH

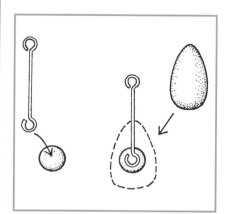

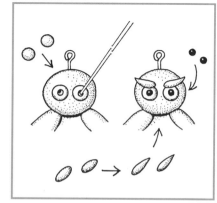

1 To make the earrings, press two 3mm (⅛ in) balls of white clay on to the board. Make a hook at the end of each eyepin with pliers and press these onto the small balls. Form two 6mm (¼ in) balls of white for the bodies, shape these into ovals and press one centrally over each flattened ball to secure the eyepins.

6 The pendant is made in the same way as the earrings, but omit the eyepins and before you apply the head, press a triangular bail into a small ball of dark brown clay positioned just below the top of the head. Proceed as for the earrings. Bake for 10 minutes. Attach a jump ring to the bail and hang the finished owl on a chain.

$\mathcal{P}$enguins are a universal favourite, and these cheeky characters make fun jewellery. You could enlarge the basic penguin design to make a pendant or a single penguin brooch. Work on both earrings at the same time so that they look the same.

MATERIALS
◆ Clay – white, black and yellow
◆ 2 SP 2.5cm (1 in) eyepins
◆ 2 SP kidney wires
◆ Brooch back
◆ Glue

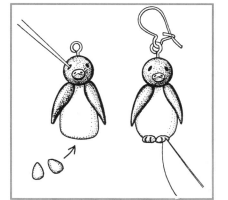

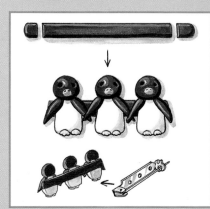

2 Roll a 6mm (¼in) log of black clay and cut four 1.5mm (¹⁄₁₆in) slices for wings. Roll the wings into ovals, point one end and press on to the bodies as above. Form 6mm (¼in) balls of black for heads and press them centrally on to the tops of the bodies. Make a 3mm (⅛in) ball of yellow, roll it into a log and point the ends. Cut it in half for the beaks, giving a flat edge to place on the penguins' faces. Make nostrils with a needle point to secure.

3 Make holes for eyes with a wool needle. Make four 3mm (⅛in) balls of yellow for the feet and point one end of each to make cones. Press these on under the penguins, pointed end to the back and mark toes with a craft knife. Bake for 10 minutes and, when cool, attach kidney wires to the eyepins.

4 To make the brooch, roll a 3mm (⅛in) log of black clay, flatten on to the board and trim to 3cm (1¼in) for a brooch bar. Make three penguins as for the dangling earrings, pressing them side-by-side on the brooch bar. Bake for 10 minutes and glue a brooch back along the brooch bar (see page 22 for gluing instructions).

5 • NOVELTY BROOCHES

Novelty brooches are the light-hearted side of jewellery, worn to bring a smile to people's faces. Children enjoy wearing novelty jewellery, of course, but many adults find it irresistible too. Because polymer clays can mimic a surprising variety of materials from lacy fabric and ribbon to metal, stone and wood – they can be used to great effect in novelty jewellery. For example, flattened sheets of clay can be draped to look like fabric such as in the design for china dolls on page 72, while squared strips of brown clay applied with a knife can mimic the timbering of the country cottages on page 78.

CIRCUS CLOWNS

*T*hese relatively simple human figures are a good project for a beginner to try. The clowns can be made in a kaleidoscope of colours, and they make lovely gifts for children.

MATERIALS
- Clay – flesh, white, black, red, green, orange and yellow
- Brooch back
- Glue

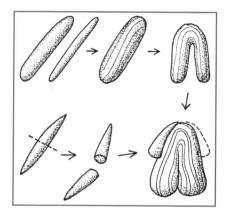

1 To make the body, marble together green and white clay (see marbling instructions on page 16). Roll a 10mm (⅜ in) log and cut a piece 3cm (1¼ in) long. Roll this longer, fold it in half and press on to the board, pushing the bottom of the legs upwards to widen them and thinning the top as above. Make the arms from a log of green 6mm (¼ in) thick. Cut a 2.5cm (1 in) length, taper both ends and cut it in half. Position the pieces on the shoulders, with the pointed ends at the top.

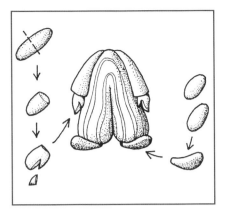

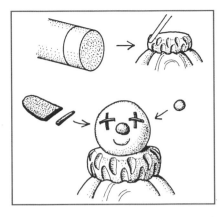

2 Form a 6mm (¼in) ball of white, shape it into an oval and cut it in half to give two hands. Flatten these slightly on the board and cut out a small wedge to make a thumb. Press on under the ends of the arms. Make two 6mm (¼in) balls of yellow for the feet. Form these into ovals and flatten them slightly, then push on under the legs, curving the toes up a little.

3 Roll a 10mm (⅜in) log of white and cut a slice 5mm (³⁄₁₆in) thick for the ruff. Press this on to the shoulders, then use a wool needle to mark indentations along the top and bottom edges. Press a 13mm (½in) ball of flesh-coloured clay on the ruff for the head. Cut thin slices from a flattened black log and use a knife to apply them in the shape of crosses for eyes. Make a smiling mouth with your needle or the end of a drinking straw. Press on a small ball of red for the nose.

4 Roll a 3mm (⅛in) log of orange and flatten it. Cut strips for hair and apply these to the head with a knife, leaving a central bald patch. Make a 3mm (⅛in) log of red and cut three slices for buttons. Press them lightly on to the front of the body and mark two holes on each with a wool needle. Bake the clown for 15 minutes and, when cool, glue a brooch back vertically on the back (see page 22).

Variations
Clowns can be made in any number of bright colours. Try varying the hair colour too. Curly hair is made by curling a thin log of clay on your finger before applying it to the head.

CHINA DOLLS

*P*retty in pastels, these little girl dolls in their Sunday best were made with transparent clay, which has a fragile, porcelain-like appearance. The results are quite delicate because the clay is rolled thin for best effect – so treat them carefully.

MATERIALS

◆ Clay – transparent, flesh, white, blue, yellow and black
◆ Tracing paper and pencil
◆ Brooch back
◆ Glue

MIXTURES

◆ Pastel blue = transparent + trace of blue
◆ Pastel yellow = transparent + trace of yellow

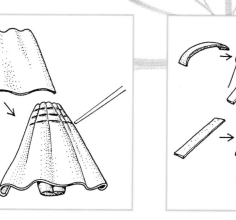

1 Form a ball of white clay, 15mm (⅝ in) in diameter, shape it into an oval and taper one end until it is 4cm (1½ in) in length. Press it on to the board, mark legs with your knife and trim to 2.5cm (1 in) long. Trace and cut out the skirt pattern. Roll out a sheet of transparent clay, about 1mm (¹⁄₃₂ in) thick, and then carefully cut out the skirt.

2 Gather the skirt in your fingers, arranging the folds and curving the side edges round to conceal them. Press the gathered edge of the skirt onto the top of the body. Mark the bodice with lines to represent smocking.

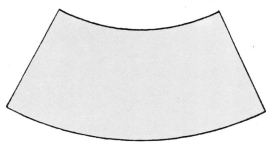

Outline for the doll's skirt

3 Roll out a strip of pastel blue clay 3mm (⅛ in) wide and 1mm (¹⁄₃₂ in) thick. Cut three lengths, placing one around the body and two trailing down. Cut a 20mm (¾ in) length and pinch it so that it is narrower in the middle and at each end. Fold the two ends to the centre to make a bow and wrap with a short piece of the strip. Press this on the front of the sash.

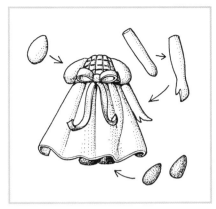

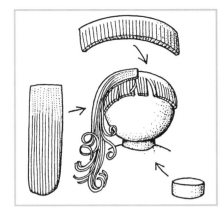

4 Form two balls of transparent clay, 6mm (¼ in) in diameter, point one end of each and press onto the sides of the bodice for puff sleeves. Roll a 5mm (³⁄₁₆ in) log of flesh-coloured clay for the arms and cut two pieces, each 20mm (¾ in) long. Round one end of each and flatten on the board. Cut out a wedge to make thumbs and position the arms on the body, with the cut edge against the sleeve. Form two 6mm (¼ in) balls of black for the feet and point one end of each slightly. Press on to the bottom of the legs, points forwards.

5 Cut a 3mm (⅛ in) length from a 3mm (⅛ in) log of flesh-coloured clay. Press on to the top of the bodice for a neck. Form a 10mm (⅜ in) ball of flesh-coloured clay for the head and press on the neck. Roll out a strip of pastel yellow, 6mm (¼ in) wide and about 1mm (¹⁄₃₂ in) thick. Cut a 13mm (½ in) length and fringe one side, curving it around the head for the fringe (bangs). Cut two 20mm (¾ in) lengths and fringe lengthwise. Position them on the sides of the head so that they meet in the middle as a parting. Curl up the ends.

6 Make two eye sockets and fill with two tiny balls of black for eyes. Form a tiny ball of flesh-coloured clay for the nose and pat in place. Indent a mouth with the tip of a wool needle. Slice the doll off the board and bake for 20 minutes. Do not bake for too long or the delicate pastel colours will discolour. When cool, glue a brooch back placed vertically on the back of the doll (see page 22).

Variations
You could use different colour schemes and hair colours. A bunch of flowers would be a pretty addition, and you can achieve a broderie anglaise effect for the dress by piercing a pattern in the rolled-out clay with a wool needle.

WIZARD

*T*his wizard has a crystal ball to help him with his magic. Use a glass stone or small marble for this, because plastic will melt when it is baked.

MATERIALS
- ◆ Clay – flesh, transparent, blue, black and violet
- ◆ Glass stone or small marble
- ◆ Small paintbrush handle or similar blunt tool
- ◆ Gold acrylic paint
- ◆ Brooch back
- ◆ Glue

MIXTURE
- ◆ Translucent blue = transparent + trace of blue + trace of violet

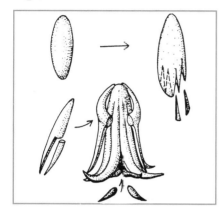

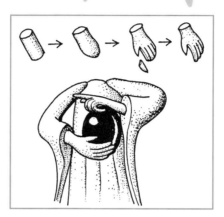

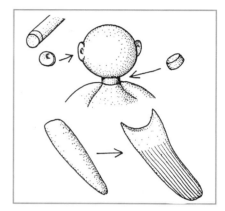

1 Roll a 6mm (¼ in) log of blue and cut a 5cm (2 in) length for the body. Form it into a 4cm (1½ in) long oval. Flatten this on the board. Use a knife to cut it as above and curve the resulting points outwards for the bottom of the gown. Mark folds with a point. Make the arms from a 6mm (¼ in) log of blue and cut a piece 2.5cm (1 in) long. Taper both ends until it is 4.5cm (1¾ in) long and cut into the above shape to give a long trailing sleeve. Position on the body, curving the arm around. Repeat for a second sleeve. Make two 6mm (¼ in) balls of black for the feet, point one end of each and insert under the folds of the gown.

2 Roll a 5mm (³⁄₁₆ in) log of flesh-coloured clay and cut two 10mm (⅜ in) lengths. Round one end of each and press the rounded end flat on the board. On each, cut away a wedge for the thumb and make three cuts for fingers. Curve the fingers round. Press the glass stone or marble onto the front of the body and curve the hands around it, placing the cut edges of the wrists against the sleeve ends.

3 Cut a 3mm (⅛ in) length from a 3mm (⅛ in) log of flesh-coloured clay and press it on to the top of the body for a neck. Press a 10mm (⅜ in) ball of the same clay on the neck for the head. Cut two thin slices of flesh-coloured clay for ears and press them to the sides of the head, indenting the centres for ear holes. Make the beard from a 6mm (¼ in) tapered log of translucent blue and roll flat. Make vertical cuts as above and trim to 20mm (¾ in) long. Pinch the top into two points and press onto the face.

HALLOWEEN WITCH

*G*lowering over her bubbling cauldron, this wicked witch is fun to make – and to wear! She is made in much the same way as the wizard.

MATERIALS
◆ Clay – black, orange, green, transparent, violet and yellow
◆ Brooch back
◆ Glue

MIXTURE
◆ Greenish flesh = transparent + trace of green

4 Make two eye sockets with a pointed tool and place a 1.5mm (¹⁄₁₆ in) ball of black clay in each. Mark wrinkles with the knife and press on a small ball of flesh-coloured clay for the nose. Apply two small pointed ovals of translucent blue for the moustache and two more for eyebrows. Roll a 10mm (⅜ in) log of blue for the hat, point one end and cut off 20mm (¾ in) from the point. Cut a slice from the top of the head and press the hat on the head, curving the point down. Bake for 20 minutes. When cool, paint a scattering of tiny gold stars over the gown and glue a brooch back on the back (see page 22).

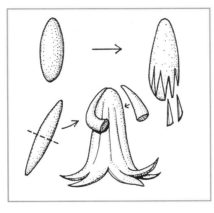

1 Make the body of black clay in the same way as the wizard on page 74. Make the arms from a 2.5cm (1 in) length of 6mm (¼ in) black log. Point the ends and cut it in half for the two arms. Arrange on the body with the pointed ends at the shoulder.

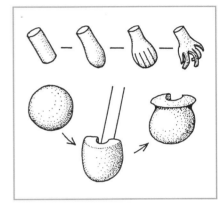

2 Roll the green flesh clay into a 3mm (⅛ in) log and cut two 6mm (¼ in) lengths for the hands. Round one end of each, leaving the other as a cut edge. Flatten the rounded end on the board and cut fingers as shown above, splaying them out and curling them under like clawing hands. Set aside until you have made the cauldron. Form a 13mm (½ in) ball of black and hollow out one side with the end of a pencil, thinning the top end and bending it over as a lip. Press the hollow side of the cauldron onto the witch's skirt.

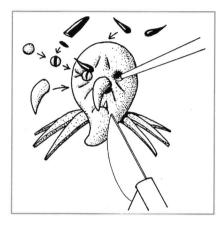

3 Arrange the hands over the cauldron, cut edges against the ends of the arms. Make flames by marbling orange and yellow. Roll the clay flat and cut spiky shapes, then press them onto the bottom of the cauldron. Roll out a sheet of black and cut pointed slices for a spiky collar. Arrange them, point side down, on top of the shoulders. Make the head from a 10mm (⅜in) ball of the green skin colour and point one end for a chin. Press the head gently on to the shoulders.

4 Mark a downwards curving mouth. Make a small cone for the nose and curve it downwards into a hook. Make two eye sockets with a point and fill with two small balls of yellow. Flatten a 1mm (¹⁄₃₂in) log and cut two slices for slit pupils, placing them on the eyeballs with your knife tip. Add wrinkles by marking the face with the tip of your knife. Two pointed ovals of black form eyebrows. Press a tiny triangle of white above the mouth for a tooth.

5 Roll out a sheet of violet clay and cut thin slices for hair, applying them over the top of the head. Form a 13mm (½in) log of black and cut a thin slice for a hat brim. Press on the top of the head. Thin the remaining log to 10mm (⅜in) and point one end. Cut off about 20mm (¾in) from the point and press the cut end on to the hat brim, bending the point as shown above. Carefully slice the witch off the board and bake for 20 minutes. When cool, glue the brooch back vertically to the back (see page 22).

BALLET SHOES BROOCH

*T*umbling ribbons decorate these dainty ballet shoes and make a brooch that would appeal to any young dancer. The photograph shows alternative colours.

MATERIALS
- Clay – red and white
- Small paintbrush handle or thick knitting needle
- Brooch back
- Glue

MIXTURES
- Pink = 1 red + 8 white
- Pale pink = 1 pink + 1 white

1 Roll the pink clay into a log 6mm (¼in) thick and cut two lengths each 4cm (1½in). Roll these again into balls and then into ovals until they form tapered logs 4cm (1½in) long. Place on the board to shape each into a slipper with a paintbrush handle. First press a trough in the centre, then thin the sides and heel and push the handle into the toe to hollow it out.

2 Form a 6mm (¼in) ball of pink into an oval and press it flat on the board for a base. Slice the shoes off the board and arrange them on top of this, the right-hand shoe pressed on the base and the left-hand shoe pressed over it at an angle. Roll a very thin log of pale pink and make a tiny bow on the front of each shoe.

3 Form the pale pink into a 1.5mm (¹⁄₁₆in) log and roll it flat until it is 3mm (⅛in) wide and about 10cm (4in) long. Cut four 2.5cm (1in) lengths and press one end of each ribbon inside the sides of the shoes. Arrange the ribbons to curl and twist over the front of the shoes. Bake for 20 minutes. When cool, glue the brooch back to the base at the back (see page 22).

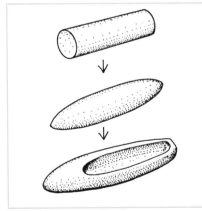

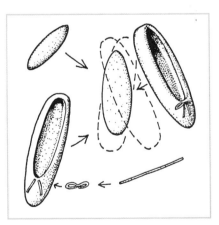

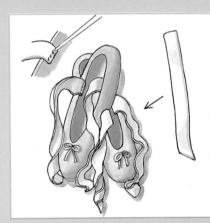

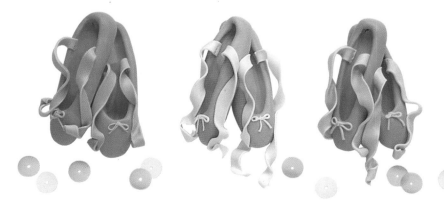

COUNTRY COTTAGE BROOCH

A half-timbered cottage with roses twining over the door makes an unusual brooch. Do not make the cottage too regular as sagging eaves and crooked timbers will add charm and give a more authentic look.

MATERIALS

- ◆ Clay – white, leaf green, light brown, dark brown, black, red, grey, blue, yellow and pink
- ◆ Brooch back or small magnet
- ◆ Glue

MIXTURES

- ◆ Roof red = 3 light brown + 1 red + 1 white
- ◆ Grass green = leaf green + yellow + white
- ◆ Pale grey = white + grey

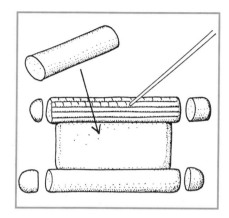

1 Roll a 6mm (¼ in) log of white, cut a piece 2.5cm (1 in) long and press onto the board to make a rectangle approximately 25 × 13mm (1 × ½in). Roll a 6mm (¼in) log of grass green, press this on under the white rectangle and trim to size. Roll a 6mm (¼in) log of roof red, press it on above the white and trim to size. Mark lines for roof tiles. Push a dip in the top to represent sagging eaves.

2 Make the chimney from a 6mm (¼in) length cut from a white 3mm (⅛in) log and press it to the top of the roof. Cut two tiny logs of roof colour and press them onto the chimney for chimney pots. Roll out a 3mm (⅛in) thick log of black to make a strip about 5mm (³⁄₁₆in) wide. Cut off two 3mm (⅛in) lengths of this and position them as windows under the roof with a knife. Mark a diamond pattern with the knife blade. Roll a 3mm (⅛ in) log of dark brown clay flat and cut thin strips for window frames, lifting them into place with your knife.

3 Cut a door, 6mm (¼ in) long, from the dark brown strip. Position it on the front of the house and mark vertical lines. Use a tiny ball of black for the door knob. Roll flat a 6mm (¼ in) log of dark brown. Cut slices of this for timbers, and position them on the wall with your knife. Aim for a rustic look by making them irregular and by placing some at angles.

4 Roll out a 1.5mm (¹⁄₁₆ in) log of leaf green for leaves and flatten it into an oval cross-section. Cut slices and apply them with the knife tip over the front door and some in flower beds. Roll logs of pink, blue and yellow, 1mm (¹⁄₃₂ in) or less thick, and cut slices for flowers, applying them among the leaves with your knife. Poke a hole in the centre of each. Paving stones are slices of pale grey. Bake the cottage for 15 minutes and, when cool, glue on a brooch back or magnet (see page 22).

Variations
Try making these in a range of styles. The basic instructions can be adapted to make thatched Suffolk pink cottages, stone Yorkshire cottages or, with a sign above the door saying 'The King's Head', a village pub. Some further ideas are shown in the photograph. They also make excellent fridge magnets.

TEDDY BEAR BROOCHES

*E*veryone loves a teddy bear! These little brooches are not difficult to make, and you can dress them up in the colours of your favourite team or add accessories for a hobby bear. If you find it difficult to make the mouths with strips of clay, you can mark in the mouth with a pen and Indian ink after baking. These instructions are for the soccer-playing teddy.

MATERIALS
◆ Clay – ochre, golden yellow, white, black and red
◆ Brooch back
◆ Glue

MIXTURE
◆ Teddy bear tan = 1 ochre + 1 yellow + white

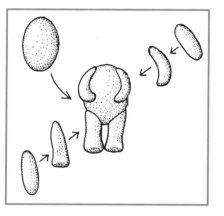

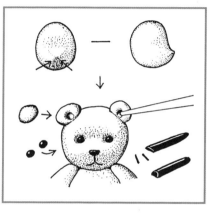

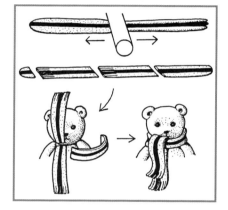

1 Form a 6mm (¼ in) thick log of the tan mixture and cut a 20mm (¾ in) length for the body. Shape it into an oval and press on the board. Cut four more lengths, 6mm (¼ in) long, and shape two into legs, wider at the bottom and with turned-up toes. Press on either side of the bottom of the body. Shape the other two into arms and press them on the sides.

2 Form a 10mm (⅜ in) ball of tan for the head and pinch out a tipped-up nose. Form two 3mm (⅛ in) balls for ears, squeeze them flat and position them on the head. Poke an ear hole in each with a wool needle, pushing the ear on to the head to secure. (If you intend to make a hat, make only one ear.) Make eye sockets and fill with two tiny balls of black. Cut a slice from a thin log of black for the nose and press it on the face. Cut very thin strips of black for the mouth and position them with the knife.

3 Make some very thin logs of red and white, about 4cm (1½ in) long, and lay them together side by side. Roll flat to make a strip 1.5mm (¹⁄₁₆ in) thick and 5mm (³⁄₁₆ in) wide. Cut two lengths of 20mm (¾ in) and fringe one end of each. Lay on the teddy, one lying upwards as above. Cut another length of scarf and wrap it around the neck. Finally bring the upper fringed piece down to look like a knotted scarf.

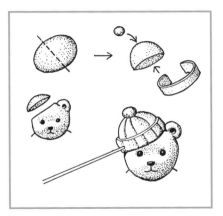

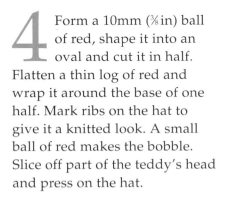

4 Form a 10mm (⅜ in) ball of red, shape it into an oval and cut it in half. Flatten a thin log of red and wrap it around the base of one half. Mark ribs on the hat to give it a knitted look. A small ball of red makes the bobble. Slice off part of the teddy's head and press on the hat.

5 To make a soccer ball, form a 3mm (⅛ in) log of white clay and another, slightly smaller, of black. Cut slices from each and arrange in the pattern above. Roll lightly to flatten. Slice off the board and wrap round a 6mm (¼ in) ball of white clay, tucking the edges under. Press under bear's paw. Bake the teddy for 15 minutes. Glue a brooch back on the back (see page 22).

Variations

The baseball player in the photograph below is made in the same way. The hat is made from a ball of blue clay and another of white, sectioned and then re-assembled, alternating the colours. A brim is pressed on the front and the whole applied to the trimmed head. The bat is a log of brown clay.

The skating teddy has white boots applied to her feet and silver painted strips of clay for skates. See page 72 for instructions on making a bow.

6 · METALLIC EFFECTS

Some spectacular effects can be obtained by using metallic powders with polymer clays. These powders are brushed on to the unbaked clay with a soft paintbrush, and, when the clay is baked and varnished, the results are similar to worked metal. Fimo produces an excellent range and Cernit has a basic range but you can use any of the metallic powders sold for craft work.

To apply the powder, place the clay on a piece of paper so that excess powder will fall on to the paper and can be re-applied. Use a soft paintbrush and stroke the powder in well. After baking, varnish with quick strokes.

Some of the following projects use artificial crystal stones to add sparkle. These are available from jewellery suppliers and craft shops, but make sure that they are made of glass to withstand baking. Plastic stones and beads can be used, but they must be added after baking.

◆ **When you work with metallic powders, avoid inhaling the dust and always work in a well-ventilated room.**

DRAGON BROOCH

This brooch has been made using four different metallic powders, but plain gold or silver would be just as striking. If you use black clay as a base, it will give a slightly antique look where it shows through.

MATERIALS
- Clay – black
- Plastic drinking straw to mark the scales (optional)
- Metallic powder – silver, blue, green and lilac
- Small crystal stone for the eye
- Brooch back
- Gloss varnish
- Glue

1 Form a log of black clay, 6mm (¼ in) thick and 11.5cm (4½ in) long. Taper one end slightly for the nose and the other more gradually into a point for the tail. Starting at the head, coil the snake of clay on the board into the shape shown below. Texture the body by marking scales all over it with the eye of a large wool needle or a drinking straw. Make cuts with a craft knife along the back of the head and curve them up into a crest.

2 Make a cut for the mouth and open it by pushing the nose up. Roll out a 1.5mm (¹⁄₁₆ in) log for the teeth, trim it to fit into the mouth and cut out teeth. Position it against the top of the mouth with your knife. Pierce a hole for the nostril. Make a hole for the eye and insert the stone. Form a tiny log for an eyebrow and press it on above the eye. Roll a long, thin tongue, split the end and trail it from the mouth across the body.

3 Form an oval with pointed ends for the forked tail and cut one end in half, curving the two ends outwards. Press it on to the tail end. Form a 6mm (¼ in) ball into an oval, point one end and press it on the board. Cut toes and curl these round into a claw. Press it to the bottom of the body. Brush the body with alternating bands of metallic powder. Dust a light covering of silver all over. Bake and varnish. Glue on a brooch back (see page 22) and glue the stone in place if it is loose.

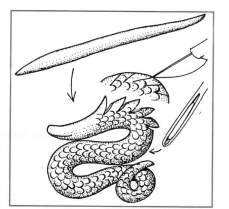

CASTLE BROOCHES

Studded with stones and sparkling with metallic powders, these fairy-tale brooches are deceptively simple to make.

MATERIALS

- Clay – white or any colour to tone with the powder
- Metallic powder – try combining two in one brooch, for example, gold and green or lilac and blue
- Artificial crystal stones for decoration
- Gloss varnish
- Brooch back
- Glue

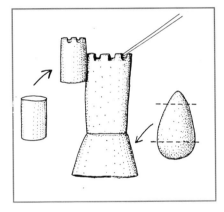

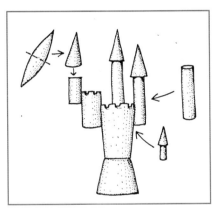

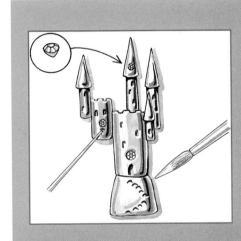

1 Roll a 6mm (¼in) log of clay and cut a 20mm (¾in) length. Press this on the board and mark crenellations with a point. Make the hill by rolling a 13mm (½in) ball of clay, making a point at one end and cutting off the top and bottom. Press on the board, the top edge against the bottom of the keep. Roll a 5mm (³⁄₁₆in) log and cut a 10mm (⅜in) length. Press this to the left-hand side of the keep and mark crenellations as before.

2 Roll a 3mm (⅛in) log and cut three different lengths. Press these on the castle, one above the keep and the other two against the sides. Make spires by rolling 6mm (¼in) balls into short logs with pointed ends, cut them in half and press each cut end on top of a tower. Make a tiny tower in the same way and press it onto the front of the castle.

3 Mark details – windows, a door and steps leading up the hill – with a wool needle. Press on the crystal stones at suitable points. Brush on metallic powder, blending it in and using different colours for the hill and spires. Bake for 10 minutes and then varnish. Glue a brooch back on the back (see page 22).

SHELL NECKLACE AND EARRINGS

$\mathcal{P}$olymer clay can be used very successfully to make highly detailed moulds from all kinds of objects – buttons, shells, nuts, jewellery, small toys and even your own clay designs. This collection of jewellery uses real shells to make polymer clay moulds. Shell moulds are particularly useful when used with metallic powders because the textures of the shells are reproduced in great detail and add to the sparkle. The resulting designs resemble shells that have been dipped into gold or silver.

Choose small shells in various shapes. A 2.5cm (1 in) cockle shell makes a good centrepiece, while small spiral shells, such as winkles or whelks, add variety. Long, thin spiral shells make the best dangling earrings.

Making Moulds

Some of the different makes of polymer clay take impressions better than others. Softer clays, such as Sculpey, are easier to use for making moulds, while the firmer clays, such as Fimo, are better for using in the mould because they are less likely to distort when you remove them. However, firmer clays can be mixed with a softening agent, such as Mix Quick, for making moulds, while the softer clays can be refrigerated inside their moulds before removal to make them firmer.

MATERIALS

◆ Clay – black and any colour for moulds
◆ Talcum powder
◆ Metallic powder – red or copper and gold for the necklace; silvers and blues for the earrings
◆ Selection of sea shells
◆ Gloss varnish

For the necklace:

◆ GP triangular or leaf bails
◆ GP jump rings
◆ GP heavy necklace chain and clasp

For the earrings:

◆ 2 SP bails or pendant mounts
◆ 2 SP fish-hook ear fittings

1 Knead the clay for the mould until it is really soft, adding mixing medium to harder clays if necessary. Shape the clay to roughly the same shape as the shell and flatten the side that is to take the impression. Smear the surface of the clay with talcum powder. Press the shell into the clay up to half way, pushing the clay against the shell's sides all round. Do not allow any overhangs to develop.

2 Carefully remove the shell from the mould, using a point to lift one side. If you have to bend the mould slightly to release the shell, bend it back to shape gently. Make moulds of the other shells. Bake the moulds for at least 30 minutes so they are really hard.

3 Knead the black clay well. Dust the inside of the mould with a paintbrush dipped in talcum powder and shake out the excess. Shape the clay roughly into the shape of the shell impression and press it in as hard as you can. With softer clays, it is easier to leave a tag of excess clay to help lifting out. Otherwise, trim off excess clay with your knife.

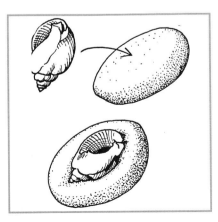

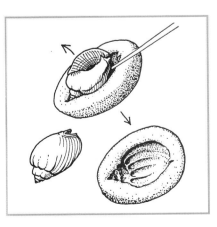

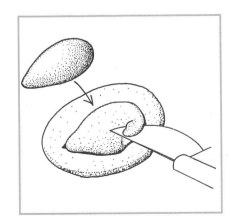

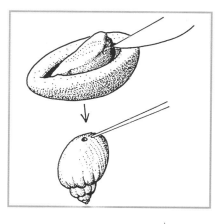

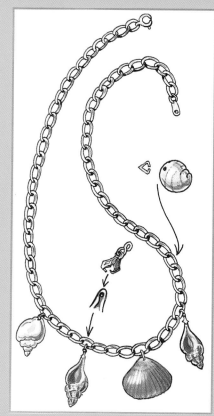

4 Push the clay away from the sides of the mould with the side of your knife and gently lift one edge. Pull out the clay. You may need a few practices with each mould to find the best way to release the clay. Lay the moulded shell on the board and trim off any excess clay. Make a small hole right through to attach the bail after baking.

5 To make the earrings, take two impressions from one mould of a long thin shell. Brush both front and back with silver and blue metallic powder or a variety of colours. Make a hole in the top of each moulded shell to take a bail or pendant mount. Bake for 10 minutes. Varnish and attach the bails and fish-hook ear wires (see page 21).

6 Make a selection of moulded shells for the necklace. Brush the front and back of the shells with gold and copper powder, using the copper inside the openings of the spiral shells and graduating the colours on the flatter shells. Bake for 10 minutes and varnish. Squeeze a bail into the hole of each shell and attach them to the chain with jump rings. Arrange the shells to hang evenly and adjust the length of the chain if necessary.

Variations
Other shell jewellery ideas are shown here. Try using coloured clay and only brushing the edges with metallic powder to obtain different effects.

SMILING SUN CHOKER AND EARRINGS

*S*miling suns and moons are eternally popular motifs, and the designs used in this and in the next project show how to model an expressive face in modelling clay. Once modelled, the designs can be moulded and reproduced for as many suns and moons as you wish.

MATERIALS
- ◆ Clay – black
- ◆ Small paintbrush handle or similar blunt tool
- ◆ Gold metallic powder
- ◆ Black velvet ribbon, 20mm (¾in) wide
- ◆ Superglue
- ◆ 2 GP ear clips or ear studs with 10mm (⅜in) flat pads
- ◆ Gloss varnish
- ◆ Fastening for choker (hooks and eyes or snap fastener)

1 Form a 10mm (⅜in) ball of black clay and press it down on the board to make a disc just under 20mm (¾in) across. Roll a 3mm (⅛in) log and wrap it around the disc, trimming the ends to meet at the bottom. Flatten this a little all round and cut points. Indent each point with the tip of the wool needle and lightly mark the position of the eyes, nose and mouth.

2 Form a small wedge shape for the nose and press this on the centre of the face, smoothing the sides into the face with the side of a needle or small modelling tool. Flatten balls of clay for the cheeks and press them on, smoothing the edges in. Indent eye sockets with a point and fill each with a small ball of clay. Roll four tiny logs with pointed ends and pat these on above and below each eye for lids. Smooth them in on the sides away from the eye.

3 Roll two tiny logs with pointed ends for the top and bottom lips and pat these on to the face, curving them upwards into a smile and smoothing the top one towards the nose for an upper lip and the bottom one towards the chin. Indent a line in the centre of the top lip and poke two nostrils in the underside of the nose. Brush the whole face with gold powder but leave the back un-gilded because turning the face over could spoil it. Bake for 10 minutes and varnish to protect the gilding when cool.

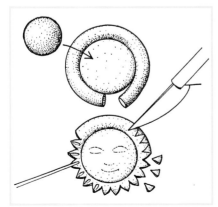

4 Roll some black clay to 1.5mm (¹⁄₁₆ in) thick and cut a bar 25 × 6mm (1 × ¼ in). Trim it so that it is slightly shorter than the width of the sun. Lay the velvet ribbon over the bar and cut two small pieces to apply to the bar ends so that the ribbon can lie between them as shown below. Bake the bar. Glue the bar vertically to the back of the sun, trapping the ribbon.

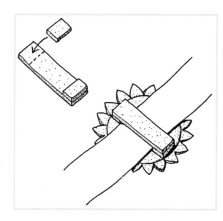

5 Neaten the ends of the choker, cutting it to fit your neck. Sew on hooks and eyes or snap fasteners. The earrings are made in exactly the same way or you can make a mould of the first sun (see instructions for making shell moulds on page 87). The points are difficult to reproduce with a mould, so it is easier to take an impression of only the face and then apply the points as above.

Glue flat pad ear fittings, either studs or clips, to the backs of the earring suns (see page 22).

MOON CHOKER AND EARRINGS

*M*ake these moons to complement your sun choker and earrings.

MATERIALS
- Clay – black
- Small paintbrush handle or similar blunt tool
- Silver metallic powder
- Black velvet ribbon, 20mm (¾in) wide
- Superglue
- 4 SP jump rings
- 2 SP fish-hook ear fittings
- Gloss varnish
- Fastening for choker (hooks and eyes or snap fastener)

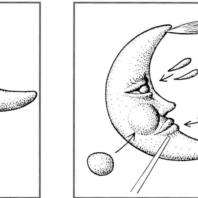

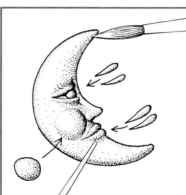

1 Form a 13mm (½in) ball of black clay and shape it into a log, 4.5cm (1¾in) long with pointed ends. Curve it into a crescent and press it down on the board. Form a nose shape and press it to the inside of the crescent, smoothing the edges into the clay with a wool needle or small modelling tool. Indent an eye socket and insert a small ball of clay. Mark a smiling mouth as a guide.

2 Roll two tiny logs, each with one end pointed, for eyelids and press on above and below the eye, blending the outer edges into the clay. Make two slightly larger logs in the same shape for the lips and press on to make a smile, again smoothing the outer edges. Apply a flattened ball for a cheek and smooth in. Brush the moon with silver powder, bake for 10 minutes and varnish when cool.

3 Make the fixing bar and choker in the same way as for the sun choker (see page 90) but angling the bar to accommodate the slant of the moon. Make two further moons for the drop earrings, either by hand or using a mould (see page 87 for moulding instructions). Pierce a hole in each just below the top point as above. After baking, attach jump rings and fish-hook ear fittings (see page 21).

Variations
Try brushing a rainbow of metallic colours across the moons' faces, or attaching dangling moons to a chain with stars for a galaxy necklace.

FISH HAIR CLIP

*S*ilvery fish are an ideal design for metallic effects because the scales add texture to the sparkling surface. Make the four fish all at the same time so that they match.

MATERIALS
- ◆ Clay – turquoise
- ◆ Plastic drinking straw for marking scales (optional)
- ◆ Metallic powders in purple, blue, green and silver
- ◆ 8cm (3¼in) long hair clip (barrette)
- ◆ Four dark blue 3mm (⅛in) rocaille beads
- ◆ Gloss varnish
- ◆ Glue

1 Roll a 10mm (⅜in) log and cut four pieces, each 20mm (¾in) long, for the fish bodies. Form each length into an oval and thin it on the right side of the middle to make the tail. Press onto the board and continue shaping, pushing the end of the tail concave. Free the tail from the board with your knife and gently bend it to curve upwards as shown below.

2 Mark scales on the fish with the end of the drinking straw or the eye of a wool needle. Roll a 6mm (¼in) log and cut four 6mm (¼in) lengths for the top fins. Shape these into long ovals with one end pointed and press them onto the top of each fish. Cut four more lengths, each 3mm (⅛in) long, and shape them into little fins. Press one onto the bottom of each fish. Mark lines on the fins and tails.

3 Cut a mouth in each fish head and open it slightly. Roll two short logs for the lips and point one end of each. Press on above and below the mouth opening. Indent an eye socket with a point and press in a rocaille bead. Slice each fish off the board and overlap them in a row. The overall measurement should be about 9cm (3½in) long.

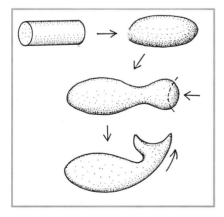

4 Brush each fish with metallic powder, coloured on the heads, blending to silver on the bodies. The turquoise clay will blend with the colour scheme and need not be completely covered. Slice the row of fish off the board and lay it on the hair clip. Bake on the hair clip for about 30 minutes. When it is cool, glue the fish to the hair clip and varnish, using plenty of varnish over the beads to secure them.

Plaited Hair Clips
These are made by plaiting ropes of clay, trimming the ends neatly and brushing a rainbow of metallic colours along the plait. Bake on the hair clip in the same way as the fish design.

STAMPED LINK BRACELET

This design uses flower stamps impressed into the clay to give a result not unlike tooled leather. The clay tiles are linked together with metal findings.

MATERIALS

- Clay – black
- Small paintbrush handle or similar blunt tool
- Metallic powders – violet, green and gold
- Gloss varnish
- GP jump rings
- GP S-fittings
- GP hook clasp

TILES TO MAKE

For an 18cm (7 in) bracelet:

- 6 square tiles
- 2 end tiles

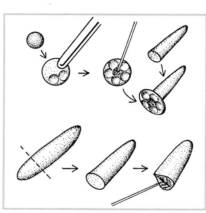

1 To make a flower stamp, form a 3mm (⅛ in) ball of clay and press it flat on the board. Using the handle of a small paintbrush or a blunt point, mark five petals and a central indentation. Prick some holes over the central indent. Make a short log for a handle, trimming one end. Make a leaf stamp by forming a short log, cut off one end and form into a leaf shape. Mark veins with a point. Bake both stamps for 10 minutes. Glue the flower stamp to the handle.

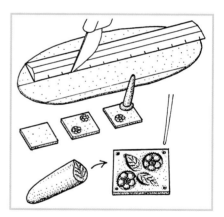

2 Roll out a sheet of black clay, a little over 1.5mm (1/16 in) thick. Using the side of the ruler as a guide, cut tiles 20 × 13mm (¾ × ½ in). Stamp each tile with two flowers and two leaves and square their edges with a straight edge if they distort. Use a wool needle to make a hole in each corner, 1.5mm (1/16 in) from each edge.

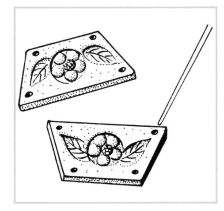

3 Make two end pieces, 20 × 8mm (¾ × ⁵⁄₁₆ in) with angled sides as above. Make holes as for the square tiles. Brush all the flowers with violet powder and the leaves with green. Finally, brush all over with gold powder. Bake for 15 minutes.

4 Varnish all the tiles. Attach an S-fitting to each hole in the tiles and link them with jump rings (see page 20). The end pieces have angled S-fittings held together by a single jump ring. Finally, attach the clasp to one end.

Enlarged detail of tiles

EGYPTIAN HIEROGLYPH NECKLACE AND EARRINGS

*T*he ancient Egyptians were highly skilled jewellers and this set is inspired by some of their designs. At this time, silver was rarer and more highly prized than gold and inscriptions in Egyptian hieroglyphs were popular for amulets.

MATERIALS
- Clay – white and scrap clay for the stamp
- Talcum powder
- Silver metallic powder
- Gloss varnish
- 14 SP 4cm (1½in) headpins
- 3 SP pendant mounts
- 6 SP jump rings
- Glass rocaille beads in turquoise and royal blue
- SP liquid silver beads
- 2 SP kidney wires
- SP chain and clasp

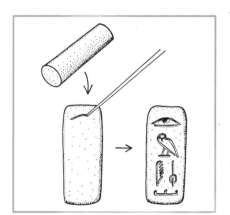

1 To make the hieroglyph stamp, form a 6mm (¼in) log from scrap clay and cut a 20mm (¾in) length. Press this on the board until it is 25 × 10mm (1 × ⅜in) and about 1.5mm (1/16in) thick. Mark the hieroglyphs as left with the point of a wool needle, incising them into the clay. Bake the stamp for 10 minutes.

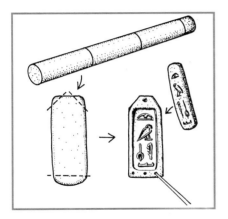

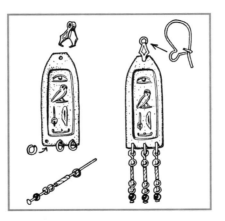

2 Form a log of white clay 8mm (⁵⁄₁₆ in) thick and cut three lengths each 2.5cm (1 in) long. Press these down on the board until they are about 3cm (1¼ in) long and 13mm (½ in) wide. Smear with talc and impress each firmly with the stamp. Trim the tops and bottoms as above. Make three holes in the bottom edge of two of the plaques (for the earrings) and one hole in the centre top of all three. Brush them with silver powder. Bake for 10 minutes and varnish.

3 To make the earrings, attach a pendant mount to the top hole of each of the plaques. Attach a jump ring to each bottom hole. Thread six headpins with rocailles and liquid silver beads in the following order: one royal blue rocaille, two turquoise rocailles, one liquid silver bead, one turquoise rocaille. Turn a loop in the top of each headpin and attach to a jump ring (see page 21). Attach kidney wires to the pendant mounts.

4 Assemble the necklace by threading four long and four short headpins with the rocailles and liquid silver beads as shown above. Trim and turn a loop in the top of each headpin. Insert a jump ring in the centre of the chain and suspend the pendant from this. Attach the headpins at even intervals from the pendant, smallest on the outside. Adjust the length of the chain if necessary to make it hang well.

CELTIC KNOTWORK
PENDANT AND EARRINGS

*T*he stunning animal designs found in the illuminated manuscripts of the seventh and eighth centuries were often repeated in the jewellery of the times. Twining snakes, birds and animals formed decorative patterns worked in gold and bronze. This set shows how well polymer clay and metallic powders can combine to mimic the ancient jewellery of Celtic and Anglo-Saxon times.

MATERIALS

- ◆ Clay – black
- ◆ Bronze metallic powder
- ◆ 1mm (½ in) or 1.5mm (¹⁄₁₆ in) rocaille beads in several colours
- ◆ 3 GP peg and loop fittings
- ◆ Gloss varnish
- ◆ 1 GP S-fitting
- ◆ 2 GP fish-hook ear wires
- ◆ 55cm (22 in) black leather thong
- ◆ 2 GP spring ends
- ◆ 1 GP hook clasp
- ◆ Superglue

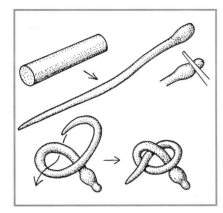

1 Form a 6mm (¼in) log of black clay and cut five pieces, each 20mm (¾in) long. Set two aside for the earrings. Roll one piece into a tapered snake 75mm (3 in) long, leaving one end with a slight bulb for the head. Roll the side of a wool needle across the bulb to make a snout and press the head down on the board to flatten it slightly. Now tie it into a knot so the head emerges from underneath the body. Repeat with the two other pieces.

2 Arrange the three serpents as above and push them gently together until you can lift each head over the body of the adjacent serpent. Press them lightly together. Make eye sockets with a point and insert tiny beads for eyes. Poke holes for nostrils. Press a small ball of clay flat on the board, lay on a peg and loop fitting and press the top of the pendant on it firmly to secure in position.

3 To make the earrings, form the remaining two pieces into serpents as before but this time, tie each knot so that the head emerges *over* the body loop. Tie the two serpents in opposite directions to make a pair. Insert beads for eyes and make nostrils in the same way. Apply a peg and loop fitting to the top back of each. Gently brush the pieces all over the surface with bronze powder.

4 Bake for 15 minutes and varnish when cool, covering the beads with varnish to secure them. Remove the peg and loop fittings from the holes, apply some glue to the hole and re-insert. Fix the spring ends to the ends of the thong and attach a clasp to one end (see page 21). Attach the pendant to the centre of the thong with the S-fitting, squeezing it tight so that it does not slip. Attach the fish-hook ear wires to the earrings (see page 21).

7 · Appliqué and Mosaic

Polymer clay appliqué is the technique of applying slices of clay to a base layer using a craft knife. Once mastered, it is a method that can produce extremely delicate work, and the results are reminiscent of cameos and Florentine mosaic. Mosaic is made in a similar way, but using small squares of clay. Appliqué and mosaics are most easily worked on a surface of smooth clay that has been pressed into a metal jewellery finding. It is also possible to work on buttons, beads, box lids, simple cushions of clay or free-form shapes, such as the appliqué kingfisher on page 106.

TIPS FOR APPLIQUÉ

◆ Never touch the slices of clay with your fingers, only with your knife or needle.

◆ Make a thin slice with your knife and scoop it up on the blade. The slight stickiness of the clay will make it stick to the knife until you turn the blade over and pat the slice on the surface of clay.

◆ There is no need to press the slices down hard; they will weld on when baked. However, avoid leaving slices sticking up too much because they will be vulnerable when the jewellery is worn. Undue pressure may also distort the smooth surface of the clay.

◆ Try not to touch the smooth clay surface you are working on; any marks on plain areas will show.

◆ The action of cutting slices will automatically distort the clay into a slight oval. This is used to advantage when cutting petals; one side of the slice will always be straighter than the other, so when you apply the petals of a flower, keep the straight edges facing in exactly the same way for symmetry.

◆ Practise the technique directly on the board to start with. Flowers can be made on the board and then transferred to the clay surface.

MOSAICS

Mosaic is the name given to the technique of building up a picture using small pieces of coloured stone, glass, ceramic clay or other materials. The earliest mosaics of baked clay and pebbles are over 5000 years old and were found in Mesopotamia, but the art of mosaic has been used by cultures as diverse as Greek, Islamic, Roman and Pre-Columbian.

Polymer clays can be used to make beautiful miniature mosaics for jewellery, and the easiest method is to build up the picture by applying small squares of clay to a smooth clay surface before baking. The squares can be applied with a knife tip in the same way as for the appliqué clay technique.

The instructions are for very tiny mosaics, but if you find this size too difficult to work with, use a larger finding and double the sizes given. You can vary the sizes of the squares, using tinier ones for the outlines or details and larger ones for the infill and background.

MINIATURE BOXES

Although miniature boxes are not worn as jewellery, they have an irresistible appeal for jewellers. There are many beautiful examples, ancient and modern, of tiny boxes studded with jewels or worked in gold, silver and enamel. It is surprisingly easy to make little boxes from modelling clay, and the results can be decorated with many of the techniques described in this book. The two examples in this chapter have mosaic applied to their lids, but you could use metallic powders, stamping, millefiori or appliqué instead.

The boxes are constructed by wrapping rolled-out clay around the base of a foil-covered miniature jam jar or similar support. You could also use an egg cup or medicine bottle, but remember that the former must be glass or ceramic so that it will withstand the low baking temperature. Do not use anything made of plastic.

ALMOND BLOSSOM BROOCH

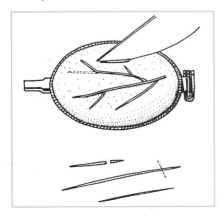

This delicate design is inspired by Chinese paintings.

MATERIALS
- Clay – transparent, dark brown, pink, black, yellow and blue
- GP milled cup brooch 20 × 13mm (¾ × ½ in)

MIXTURES
- Beige = transparent + trace of dark brown
- Pale pink = transparent + pink
- Pale blue = transparent + blue

1 Carefully fill the brooch with beige clay, following the instructions on page 105. Roll out a very thin log of dark brown and cut pieces for the branch, pointing the ends and lifting each piece into place with your knife.

2 Roll a 1.5mm (¹⁄₁₆ in) log of transparent clay and cut tiny slices for petals, giving each flower five petals and radiating them around a central point for each. Mix a little pink with transparent clay and roll a 1mm (¹⁄₃₂ in) log. Cut and place a slice in the centre of each flower for the stamen section and several on the ends of the branches for the buds. Poke a small hole in the centre of each flower with a wool needle.

3 Form a 1.5mm (¹⁄₁₆ in) log of black and cut a slice for the bee's body. Roll the log thinner and cut a slice for the head. Flatten a thin yellow log slightly and cut a strip, positioning it across the centre of the body. Roll a thin log of pale blue and cut a slice for each wing as below. Pat the design lightly all over with your finger and bake, in its finding, for about 10 minutes. Glue the clay into the finding if it is not already firmly set.

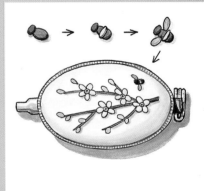

Variations
The iris and dragonfly brooch shown above is made with long slices of marbled violet and transparent clay for the irises and leaves as for the bluebell leaves on page 105. The dragonfly is simply slices of flattened blue and black log.

DAISY EARRINGS

*B*right-eyed daisies with rosy tips to their petals make appealing earrings. You could make a matching pendant using the same techniques.

MATERIALS
- Clay – white, transparent, blue, leaf green, crimson and yellow
- 2 SP round milled cup earrings, 10mm (⅜ in) diameter.

MIXTURES
- Pale blue = transparent + trace of blue
- Pink = white + crimson

1 Carefully fill the cup earrings with pale blue clay, following the instructions on page 105. Push the posts of the earrings into a block of clay to steady them while you work. Roll a 3mm (⅛ in) leaf green log and press it into an oval cross-section. Cut and apply three leaves to each earring and then mark veins with a knife.

2 Roll the pink clay into a 1.5mm (⅟₁₆ in) log. Roll a white log, 3mm (⅛ in) thick, and lay the pink log along it. Roll both together into a 1.5mm (⅟₁₆ in) log, which will now be largely white with a pink streak. Position the pink streak at one side and press the log into a thin cross-section so that the pink streak becomes the petal's pink tip. Slice the petal log and apply the petals in a daisy shape, radiating from a central point and with the pink tips outwards.

3 Make two daisies for each earring, the second slightly overlapping the first. Cut small slices from a 1.5mm (⅟₁₆ in) yellow log for the flower centres and prick with a pin to create the texture. Bake for about 10 minutes. Glue the clay into the findings if it is slightly loose to secure.

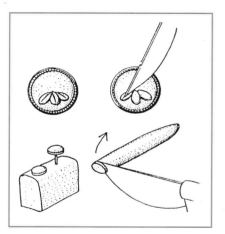

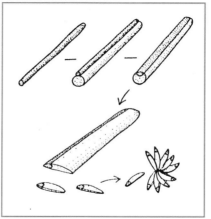

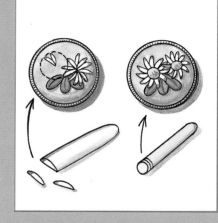

BLUEBELL PENDANT

*T*ransparent clay is used as a base layer for this brooch to give a delicate, porcelain quality. Instead of using a silver-plated finding, try a real silver one – the results are worth the small extra expense.

MATERIALS
- Clay – transparent, leaf green, blue, violet, yellow and black
- Silver milled cup pendant, 20 × 13mm (¾ × ½ in)
- Silver chain

MIXTURES
- Bluebell blue = blue + transparent + violet
- Primrose yellow = yellow + transparent

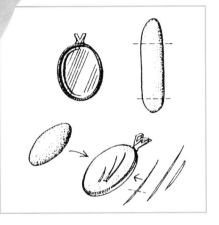

1 Form transparent clay into a log that is slightly narrower than the width of the finding. Cut a length equal to the pendant. Roll this into an oval and press it into the cup until it reaches the edges all round. The top surface should be just level with the rim. Stroke the surface of the clay with your finger until it is smooth. Roll the leaf green into thin logs with pointed ends. Cut five lengths, the longest about 13mm (½ in), and lift with your knife onto the prepared transparent clay, curving the tops over slightly.

2 Roll the bluebell blue clay into a log 1mm (¹⁄₃₂ in) thick, flatten slightly and cut slices for the bluebells, applying them to the stalks. Roll a log of leaf green about 1.5mm (¹⁄₁₆ in) thick and press it lightly to give an oval cross-section. Cut six thin slices and arrange to cover the base of the bluebell stalks and leaves. Mark veins with the knife tip.

3 Roll a 1.5mm (¹⁄₁₆ in) log of primrose yellow clay and cut tiny slices for primrose petals, lifting each into place on your knife and radiating them out, five to each flower. Pierce the centre of each flower with a wool needle. Cut four tiny slices of blue for the butterfly wings and arrange them as above. A tiny slice of black forms the body. Bake the clay in the finding for 10 minutes, then, when it is cool, glue the clay in place if it is not firmly secured.

KINGFISHER BROOCH

The appliqué technique can be used successfully to mimic the fluttering feathers of birds. The glorious colours of a kingfisher are captured by the use of acrylic paint on this striking brooch.

Outline for the kingfisher's body and wings

Upper wing   Lower wing   Body

MATERIALS

- ◆ Baking parchment and pencil
- ◆ Clay – transparent
- ◆ Nail varnish remover
- ◆ Artists' acrylic paints – black, orange, turquoise, white and blue
- ◆ Matt varnish
- ◆ Gloss varnish
- ◆ Brooch back
- ◆ Glue

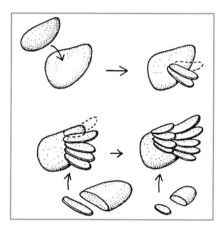

1 Trace the outlines on to a sheet of baking parchment. Form a 8mm (5/16 in) ball of transparent clay, roll it into an oval and press it down on the traced upper wing outline, pushing it into shape. Flatten a 6mm (1/4 in) log until it is 3mm (1/8 in) thick. Cut slices and apply with your knife to the wing, starting halfway up and working towards the tip. Roll a 3mm (1/8 in) log and flatten it in the same way. Cut and apply slices for the smaller feathers, overlapping the first row.

2 Roll a 10mm (3/8 in) log and cut a 13mm (1/2 in) length for the body, a 6mm (1/4 in) length for the head and a 3mm (1/8 in) length for the tail. Form all three pieces into ovals and press them down on the body outline, making the tail flatter than the other pieces. Smooth the joins with a wool needle or modelling tool. Slice the body off the board with the knife and press it down on the upper wing, using the outline as a guide.

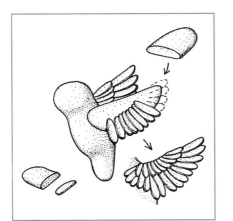

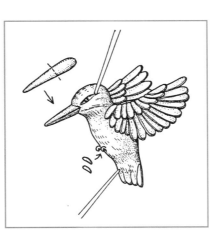

3 Make the lower wing from a 13mm (½in) length of 6mm (¼in) log and re-roll it into an oval 2.5cm (1 in) long. Press this on the lower wing outline, curving it into shape. Slice off the board and press it on the body, curving it over the upper wing. Apply large feathers as before, starting with a few to hide the join with the body and working round to the wing tip. Repeat with smaller feathers, placing them to cover the tops of the large feathers.

4 Apply one long feather to the back of the tail and a few smaller ones at the bottom, smoothing the tops into the body. Texture the head and body with small marks. Roll a pointed log of clay and cut off 13mm (½in) from the point for the beak. Press it to the head and smooth the join. Mark a line along the beak. Form two tiny ovals for the feet, press on with the wool needle and curve the tops over. Pierce an eye socket and insert a tiny ball of clay. Mark a 'brow' line.

5 Bake the kingfisher for 20 minutes. When it is cool, brush all over with nail varnish remover to remove all traces of grease. Paint the bird in the colours shown above, grading the feathers from turquoise to blue at the tips. Leave the paint to dry overnight and then apply a coat of matt varnish to protect the paint. Put a drop of gloss varnish onto the eye. Glue on a brooch back (see page 22).

ROMAN VASE PENDANT

*T*his elegant vase motif was popular with the Romans, who adorned many of their villas with spectacular mosaic floors.

MATERIALS

- ◆ Clay – white, black, crimson, blue, yellow, green and transparent
- ◆ Tracing paper and pencil
- ◆ Gloss or matt varnish
- ◆ Silver milled cup pendant 20mm × 13mm (¾ × ½ in)
- ◆ Silver chain

MIXTURES

- ◆ Purple = small quantity of blue + crimson
- ◆ Pink = small quantity crimson + white
- ◆ Transparent blue = blue + transparent
- ◆ Dark green = blue + green

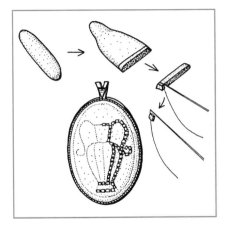

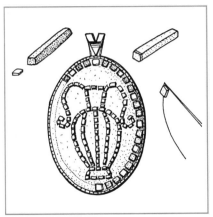

1 Fill the finding with white clay following instructions on page 105. Trace the outline on to tracing paper, cut it out and press it on the surface of the clay. Mark the lines with a pin so that they indent the clay lightly. Form a 6mm (¼ in) log of black and roll it flat until it is about 1mm (¹⁄₃₂ in) thick. Cut a strip of this, 1.5mm (¹⁄₁₆ in) wide, and press it lightly on the board to keep it steady. Cut tiny rectangles from the end of the strip and apply them with your knife to the outline.

2 Make larger, 1.5mm (¹⁄₁₆ in), strips of purple, pink, yellow and dark green in the same way and apply 1.5mm (¹⁄₁₆ in) squares around the outside of the pendant, alternating the colours. Start at the top and work down each side, making sure that the sides match.

3 Marble together blue and transparent clay and make 1mm (¹⁄₃₂ in) squares as above. Apply these in lines between the vase outline. Cut white squares for the background, aligning them with the border in concentric circles outside the vase and filling the area inside the handles. Finally, add a few thin black squares on top of the white squares inside the handles to continue the curl. Bake for 10 minutes and varnish sparingly with matt or gloss varnish to protect the mosaic.

Outline for the Roman vase mosaic

LOVE KNOT BOX

*T*his delicate design has a timeless appeal, and the love knot in the centre was frequently used in Roman mosaics. The box and lid are made of transparent clay, which gives a porcelain effect.

MATERIALS

- ◆ Clay – transparent, leaf green, pink, black and dark brown
- ◆ Small jar or egg cup, about 3.5cm (1⅜ in) in diameter, to use as a former for the box
- ◆ Aluminium foil
- ◆ Talcum powder
- ◆ Tracing paper and pencil
- ◆ Gloss varnish

MIXTURES

- ◆ Beige = white + trace of dark brown
- ◆ Translucent pink = transparent + pink

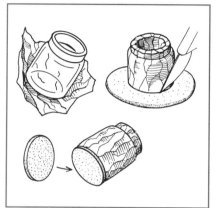

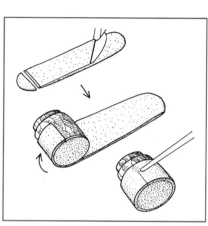

1 Cover the jar with aluminium foil and smooth out the wrinkles as much as possible. Roll out some transparent clay to 1.5mm (¹⁄₁₆ in) thick and stand the jar on the clay sheet. Holding your knife vertically, cut out the shape of the jar's bottom. Press this base disc onto the foil.

2 Roll out another sheet of clay to 1.5mm (¹⁄₁₆ in) thick. Trim to make a piece approximately 4 × 10cm (1½ × 4 in), depending on the size of your jar. Lay the jar on its side on the sheet so that the trimmed long side is in line with the base disc. Roll the jar up in the sheet, trimming the edges flush and keeping the bottom edge in line with the base disc all round. Smooth the joins with a knife or modelling tool.

Outline for love knot box mosaic

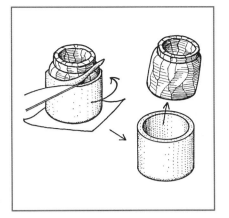  

3 Stand the jar on a small piece of baking parchment so you can rotate it easily, and hold the knife horizontally against the clay as you turn the jar to trim the top edge. Bake for 10 minutes and allow to cool for a few minutes. Remove the box carefully from the jar by twisting and pulling it away with the foil.

4 Roll out a sheet of transparent clay, 3mm (⅛ in) thick, on a piece of baking parchment. Brush the surface well with talcum powder and press the box, opening downwards, onto the clay until it has made an impression 1.5mm (⅟₁₆ in) deep. Holding the box on to the impression and, with your knife held vertically, cut out the lid. Remove the waste clay and transfer the lid, still on the parchment, to the baking sheet. Bake for 10 minutes. Check that the lid fits the box well, trimming away any clay, if this is necessary.

5 Roll out a 1.5mm (⅟₁₆ in) sheet of transparent clay and lay the lid, top down on it. Cut round it with the knife. Carefully apply the resulting clay disc to the top of the lid, smoothing the joins all round the edge. You are now ready to decorate the lid. Trace the design from the template, lay the tracing paper on top of the lid and mark the lines with a pin to transfer the design to the soft clay.

6 The mosaic design is made using 1.5mm (¹⁄₁₆ in) squares. Roll flat a 6mm (¼ in) log of black clay until it is 1.5mm (¹⁄₁₆ in) thick. Cut several 1.5mm (¹⁄₁₆ in) strips. Now cut thin slices from the ends of the strips to give tiny squares. Apply these with the knife tip to the outline design on the clay surface, aligning all the squares very carefully.

7 Use the same technique with the other colours, filling in the flower outlines with pink and the knot outline with beige. The leaves are outlined with green before filling them in around the central rib of black. Cut slightly larger squares of transparent clay for the background. Apply them around the edge of the box and work inwards, keeping the lines of squares in concentric circles. Bake the finished lid for 10 minutes. Varnish the whole box with gloss varnish. If you wish, paint the inside of the box smoothly with acrylic paint for decorative finish.

SAILING SHIP BOX

*T*his little box depicts a caravel sailing ship of the kind that was used by Christopher Columbus. The box is made of white clay, but you could use marbled browns instead to give the impression of turned wood. If you choose to do this, use white instead of transparent clay for the sky mixture; otherwise the brown would show through.

MATERIALS
- Clay – white, transparent, dark brown, black, yellow, blue and turquoise
- Small jar or egg cup, about 3cm (1¼ in) in diameter, to use as a former for the box
- Aluminium foil
- Talcum powder
- Tracing paper and pencil
- Gloss varnish

MIXTURES
- Sky blue = transparent + trace of blue
- Sea blue = white + blue
- Cream = white + trace of brown
- Gold = yellow + trace of brown

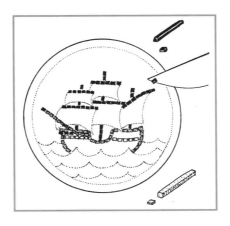

1 Follow the instructions for the love knot box on page 110, making the box and lid with white clay and applying a white disc to the top of the baked lid. Trace the outline and transfer the design to the soft clay in the same way. Roll out black clay to 1mm (½2 in) thick and make squares for the masts and spars (see page 112, step 6). Outline the hull in brown and fill in, adding a line of gold.

2 Apply turquoise squares to outline the waves and then a line of blue, filling in between with sea blue. The sails are mainly cream, with some white to highlight them and brown to define the sides. Finally, fill in the background with larger squares of sky blue. Bake the lid for 10 minutes and varnish the whole box. The inside of the box can be painted in a contrasting colour with acrylic paint.

Outline for sailing ship mosaic

8 · BUTTONS

Polymer clay is absolutely ideal for making your own buttons. After baking, the clay is washable up to 40°C (104°F) and can even be washed in a washing machine. Hand knitters can make buttons that are exactly the right size and colour to match their work, while home dress-makers need never be at a loss for just the right buttons. You can invigorate a garment with novelty buttons or make a colour mixture to blend perfectly – the possibilities are endless.

Many of the techniques described in previous chapters can be used to decorate buttons. Stamping, metallic powders, marbling, millefiori and painting can all be applied very successfully.

BASIC TIPS

◆ Keep button designs as smooth as possible. A wonderful-looking design that will not pass easily through the buttonhole is extremely irritating. Small threads can catch on sharp edges or protuberances, so try to keep these to a minimum.

◆ As long as a button is smooth, it does not have to be round. Asymmetrical buttons are perfectly functional and offer new design possibilities.

◆ Always make the holes big enough for sewing the button to a garment. It is best to make a small dip between the holes in which the thread can lie to prevent it from becoming worn.

◆ Polymer clay buttons are best made with holes right through them. It is possible to glue a shank to the back of the button, but this will not be as strong.

◆ All polymer clay buttons can be washed by hand and most can be machine washed to 40°C (104°F). If you paint or varnish your buttons, it is safest to hand-wash.

◆ Bake buttons for 20–30 minutes to harden them as much as possible.

NOVELTY BUTTONS

Novelty buttons are always popular with children, and polymer clay can be used to make a wonderful variety of lively novelty buttons that will give home-made clothes a sparkling individuality. Two designs are given at the end of this chapter, but do try experimenting with your own ideas. Some of the designs in the earlier chapters on animal jewellery and novelty brooches can be adapted to make buttons, especially the pig earrings, the penguins and the clowns. Make the buttons flatter and smoother than the jewellery and avoid any legs or ears that stick out, because they may catch or be broken off in use.

MAKING A BASIC ROUND BUTTON

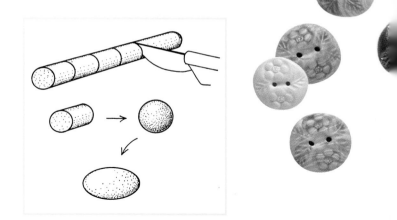

Forming the button

Roll a 6mm (¼in) log of clay and cut equal lengths. As a guide, 6mm (¼in) lengths will give 13mm (½in) buttons, and 13mm (½in) lengths will give 15mm (⅝in) buttons. Form each length into a ball and press it down on the board with a flat finger-tip, keeping the button as circular as possible. The best thickness for most buttons is approximately 3mm (⅛in).

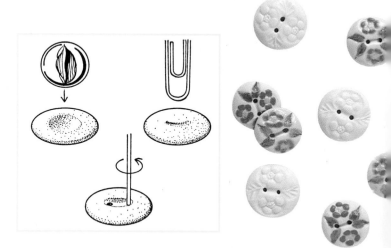

Piercing the button

Indent the centre of the button using a marble, the edge of a coin, a pen cap or the end of a paperclip, depending on the effect you want. Pierce holes in the button with a wool needle, enlarging them slightly by rotating the needle in the hole.

OAK LEAF STAMPED BUTTONS

*O*nce you have mastered the technique of making simple round buttons, you can decorate them in a variety of ways. Stamping is an effective form of decoration because, once you have made a stamp, impressing a pattern is quick and easy.

MATERIALS
- Clay – golden-yellow, white and scrap clay for the stamp
- Talcum powder
- Brown powder paint or artists' pastel
- Small plastic button
- Superglue
- Matt acrylic varnish

MIXTURE
- Biscuit = 1 golden yellow + 7 white

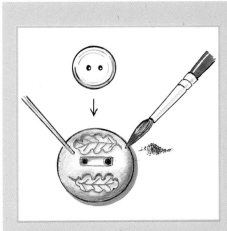

1 To make the oak leaf stamp form a 3mm (⅛in) ball of scrap clay into an oval and press it on the board to make a leaf shape. Use a blunt wool needle to make indentations all round, pushing the tip of the needle into the side of the leaf. Mark veins. Form a short log for a handle and cut off one end. Bake the oak leaf and handle for about 10 minutes. When they are cool, glue the oak leaf to the cut end of the handle.

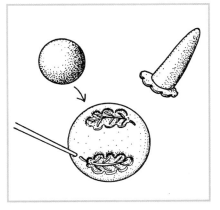

2 Roll the biscuit clay into a 6mm (¼in) log and cut 13mm (½in) lengths. Make these into plain round buttons (see page 116). Dust the buttons with talc and press the oak leaf stamp into the top and bottom of each button. Mark a small stalk.

3 Make a channel for the thread by impressing the edge of a small plastic button into the centre of each button, then make two holes with a wool needle. With a soft paintbrush, dust the edges of the oak leaf impressions and the edges of the buttons with brown powder. Bake for approximately 30 minutes and, when cool, varnish with matt varnish.

Variations
The floral buttons opposite have been made using the stamps described on page 94. They were then either left plain, or the design was picked out in acrylic paint, or it was brushed with metallic powder.

MARBLED BUTTONS

$\mathscr{M}$arbling is simple to do but gives versatile buttons. You can choose any toning or contrasting mixture of colours to match your garment. Wood-effect buttons can be made by marbling different browns together, or you can add transparent clay instead of a colour to give translucent streaks.

MATERIALS

◆ Clay – several colours of your choice

◆ Pen top, glass marble, coin or paper clip for indenting

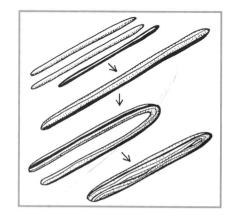

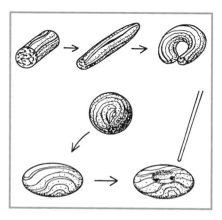

1 Roll 3mm (⅛in) logs of each colour, lay them together and roll into a thinner log. Fold in half and roll again, continuing until you have a pleasing marbled effect of longitudinal streaks. Make sure you marble sufficient clay to make all your buttons at the same time because it will be difficult to match the effect. As a guide, three 10cm (4 in) lengths of 3mm (⅛in) log marbled together gives enough for six 13mm (½in) buttons.

2 Cut the marbled log into equal lengths of the size required and roll each length again to make it longer. Curl it round to tuck in the cut edges and roll into a ball. Choose the side of the marbling you wish to have uppermost and press each ball down on the board. Follow the instructions on page 116 for making basic buttons.

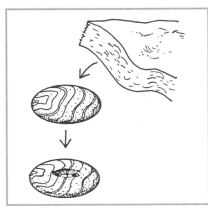

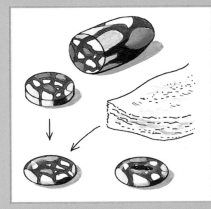

Rough-textured or Granite-textured marbled buttons

These are made with the same texture as the granite beads on page 33. Marble the clay and make the basic round button shapes. Press a small piece of quilt wadding down on each button to give it a 'granite' texture but take care not to distort the round shape. Make holes and bake following the instructions for basic buttons (see page 116).

Surprise Buttons

These buttons are made with left-over first-stage canes from millefiori – the resulting accidental designs are always a surprise. Squash together the ends of millefiori canes to form a ball, adding any extra colours if you wish. The canes shown used white, leaf green, yellow and orange clay wrapped with black plus a few extra colours. Roll them into a fat log, about 13mm (½in) thick. Cut off the end to square it and cut 3mm (⅛in) slices. Press these on the board, texture with wadding and make the holes as on page 116. Bake for 30 minutes.

Rainbow Millefiori Buttons

*M*illefiori canes be be made into buttons by cutting 3mm (⅛ in) slices from the patterned cane, pressing them down on the board and making holes. This youthful design looks wonderful on children's dungarees. Alternative colour schemes are shown in the photograph but try designing your own canes and colour variations.

MATERIALS
- ◆ Clay – white, blue, crimson, orange, yellow, green and violet
- ◆ Razor blade for slicing the canes

MIXTURES
- ◆ Light blue = 3 white + 1 blue
- ◆ Light green = 1 green + 1 yellow
- ◆ Dark green = 2 green + 1 blue

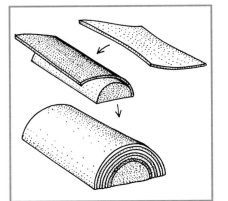

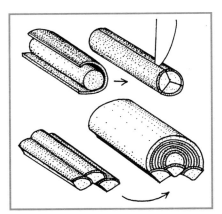

1 Roll a 6mm (¼ in) log of light blue clay, trim to 5cm (2 in) long and press down on the board until it has a semi-circular cross-section. Roll out 1.5mm (¹⁄₁₆ in) sheets of violet, blue, green, yellow, orange and crimson clays and apply them, in that order, to the light blue, tucking the edges of each down against the sides and trimming to fit. Finish with a thicker layer of light blue.

2 Form a 6mm (¼ in) log of light green, 5cm (2 in) long, and wrap a 1.5mm (¹⁄₁₆ in) sheet of dark green around it. Cut this into three lengthwise sections. Pile the sections on to each other, dark green sides uppermost so they nest together and look like hills. Press the hills onto the bottom of the rainbow.

3 Roll the cane on the board to make it round in section and firm all the colours together. Continue rolling until it is 13mm (½ in) thick. Cut 3mm (⅛ in) slices and lay them on the board. Push any distortion from the cutting back into shape and press down with the flat of your finger until they are nicely rounded. Indent and make the holes as described on page 116. Bake for 30 minutes.

TURKISH CARPET MILLEFIORI BUTTONS

*M*otifs of simple triangles and diamonds are used in many different cultures, from the Middle East to Africa and the Americas. This design was suggested by carpet weaving. All the buttons shown here were made using different colour ways of the same design, and they show how changing the colours can change the design dramatically. The technique used is for square-section millefiori, which is more suitable for geometric patterns because it will distort them less than using round canes.

MATERIALS
◆ Clay – dark brown, yellow, leaf green and orange
◆ Razor blade for slicing the canes

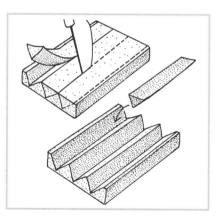

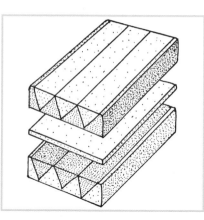

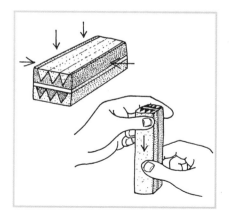

1 Roll out a sheet of yellow clay until it is 5mm (³⁄₁₆ in) thick. Trim it to 25 × 40mm (1 × 1½ in). Holding the knife at an angle, cut out three wedges of triangular cross-section. Roll out a sheet of leaf green clay of the same thickness and cut three triangular wedges of the same size. Insert these wedges into the spaces left in the yellow clay.

2 Roll out a sheet of yellow clay to 1.5mm (¹⁄₁₆ in) thick, trim it to the same size and press it on top of the green triangles. Now repeat step 1, this time using dark brown and orange clay. Then press this second layer on top of the yellow and green layer.

3 Reduce the cane by pressing it down on the board along its length and then squeezing it back into a square cross-section. After doing this a few times, slice it from the board and hang it vertically in one hand. Stroke your other hand down the length, gently stretching it longer but still keeping the square section. Return it to the board as necessary to square up.

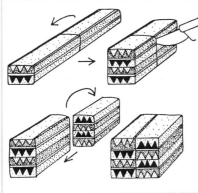

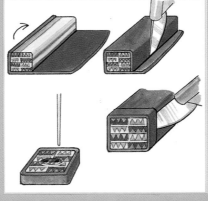

4 When the cane is about 10mm (⅜in) across, trim the distorted ends and cut it in half, placing one half over the other. Cut in half again, turn one half upside down and place it alongside the first. Reduce the cane again until it is 13mm (½in) thick or the size you require for the buttons.

5 Roll a 1.5mm (¹⁄₁₆in) sheet of dark brown and wrap it around the cane, trimming the edges to fit. Stroke the cane all over to firm the clay together. Cut 3mm (⅛in) slices for the buttons, lay them on the board and press with your finger to flatten them. Keep the overall square shape but allow the corners to round slightly. Make holes as described on page 116. Bake for 30 minutes.

Variations
The photograph above shows several different colour schemes. The cane can be made with only black and white for the triangular wedges; you can then wrap the final cane with more than one layer of colour.

SOLDIER TOGGLES

*T*oggles are popular fastenings for children's anoraks and coats because they are easy for small fingers to do up. These bright little soldiers will make that task far more entertaining. It is best to make the soldiers all at the same time in a row so that you can check that they match.

MATERIALS
- ◆ Clay – black, red, golden-yellow and flesh

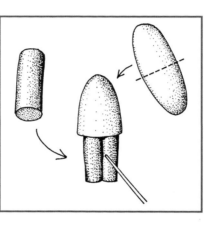

1 Roll a log of black clay 6mm (¼in) thick and cut as many 13mm (½in) lengths as you need toggles. Press these on the board for the legs and mark a central line. Roll a 10mm (⅜in) log of red and cut 20mm (¾in) lengths. Form into ovals 3cm (1¼in) long and cut each in half to give two bodies. Press firmly over the tops 8mm of the legs.

2 Roll a 6mm (¼in) log of red clay and cut 13mm (½in) lengths. Re-roll each until it is 3cm (1¼in) long, with tapered ends, and cut in half to give two arms. Press these on the body. Form a small oval of flesh-coloured clay and cut it in half to give two hands. Press these on the bottom of the arms. Roll a 10mm (⅜in) ball of flesh and press it on the body for the head.

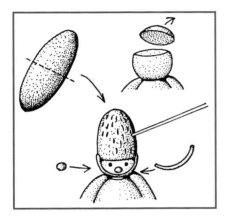

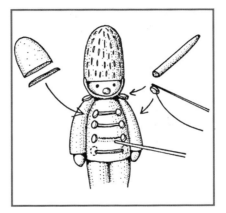

3 Roll a 13mm (½ in) ball of black clay and form it into an oval, 2.5cm (1 in) long. Cut it in half to make two helmets and flatten them slightly on the board. Trim the top of the head and press on the helmet. Mark lines for fur. Roll a thin log of black for a strap and attach under the chin. Press on a small ball of flesh for the nose and indent two eyes.

4 Roll flat a 3mm (⅛ in) log of yellow and cut slices for trimming, applying three horizontally to the body, leaving a gap at the waist to mark a thread channel. Cut slices from a 3mm (⅛ in) log of yellow for buttons and place as above, with one at each end of the thread channel too. Position a slice of yellow on each shoulder for epaulettes.

5 Form a 6mm (¼ in) ball of black into an oval and cut it in half for two feet. Press firmly onto the bottom of the legs, cut edges to the back. Make a hole through the toggle at the each end of the thread channel. Check that everything is firmly pressed on because the toggles will receive heavy wear. Bake for 30 minutes. Sew the toggles on with strong yellow thread so that the trimming is complete.

SILVERED FISH BUTTONS

*T*his design looks stunning against black mohair knitwear. The sizes given make buttons about 13mm (½ in) across, but you could double the measurements to make them much larger. The open end of a ball-point pen refill is a useful implement for suggesting scales.

Actual size

MATERIALS
- ◆ Clay – blue or black
- ◆ Small paintbrush handle or similar tool
- ◆ Ball-point pen refill or similar tube for marking scales
- ◆ Metallic powders– silver, blue and violet
- ◆ Gloss varnish

Double size

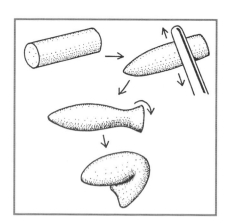

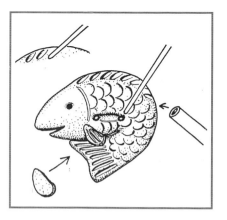

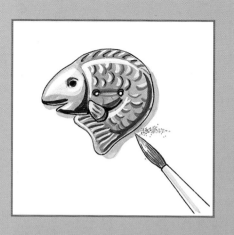

1 Roll a 6mm (¼ in) log of clay and cut 13mm (½ in) lengths. Roll one end of each into a point and thin the clay two-thirds of the way along for the tail by rolling a paintbrush handle across the clay. Pinch the tail flat and then curve it round under the head. Press the fish flat on the board.

2 Mark the details with a wool needle, pressing lines over the top of the fish for a dorsal fin. Mark scales with the ball-point pen refill. Cut a mouth and mark an eye. Cut a small slice for a fin, press it on the body and mark it with lines. Make two holes in the centre of the fish and depress the clay between them slightly for a thread channel.

3 Brush the buttons with metallic powder – silver on the head and blue and violet on the body. Bake for 30 minutes. Varnish with gloss varnish to protect the surface.

FURTHER READING

Dierks, Leslie, *Creative Clay Jewelry*, Lark Books, Asheville, North Carolina, 1994

Ford, Steven and Dierks, Leslie, *Creating with Polymer Clay: Designs, Techniques and Projects*, Lark Books, Asheville, North Carolina, 1996

Heaser, Sue, *Making Doll's House Miniatures with Polymer Clay*, Ward Lock, London 1997

Kato, Donna, *The Art of Polymer Clay*, Watson Guptill, New York 1997

Maguire, Mary, *Polymer Claywork*, Lorenz Books, London 1996

Roche, Nan, *The New Clay*, Flower Valley Press, Rockville, Maryland, 1991

SUPPLIERS AND ORGANIZATIONS

Polymer clays are available in craft and art material shops and also by mail order from craft, jewellery and bead suppliers. If you have problems finding the clays, the following suppliers should be able to help.

AUSTRALIA

Staedtler (Pacific) Pty Ltd
PO Box 576
Inman Road
Dee Why
NSW 2099
(Fimo)

C.A.M.
197 Blackburn Road
Syndal
VIC 3149
(Modelene)

Rossdale Pty Ltd
137 Noone Street
Clifton Hills
VIC 3068
(Sculpey III, Premo)

CANADA

Staedtler Mars Ltd
6 Mars Road, Etobicoke
Ontario M9V 2KI
(Fimo)

KJP Crafts
PO Box 5009 Merival Depot
Nepean
ONT K2C 3H3
(Sculpey, Premo)

NEW ZEALAND

Golding Handcrafts
PO Box 9022
Wellington
(Du-Kit, Fimo)

New Image Art Supplies Ltd
23 Woodside Road
Mount Eden
Auckland
(Sculpey, Premo)

UNITED KINGDOM

Inscribe Ltd
Woolmer Industrial Estate
Bordon
Hampshire GU35 9QE
(Fimo)

CATS Group
PO Box 12
Saxmundham
Suffolk IP17 3PB
(Cernit)

Specialist Crafts
PO Box 247
Leicester LE1 9QS
(will export Formello worldwide)

Edding (UK) Ltd
Merlin Centre, Acrewood Way
St Albans
Hertfordshire AL4 0JY
(Sculpey, Premo)

UNITED STATES

American Art Clay Co Inc
4717 W. Sixteenth Street
Indianapolis, 46222-2598
(Fimo)

Clay Factory of Escondido
PO Box 460598
Escondido
CA 92046-0598
(Cernit, Sculpey III, Premo)

POLYMER CLAY ORGANIZATIONS
(please send a s.a.e. when enquiring about membership)

The British Polymer Clay Guild
Meadow Rise
Wortham, Diss,
Norfolk IP22 1SQ
UK

The National Polymer Clay Guild
Suite 115-345
1350 Beverly Road
McLean, VA 22101
USA

Current information on suppliers can be found on the World Wide Web site:
http://www.heaser.demon.co.uk

INDEX